Josh Moody

John 1–12

Life to the Full

GOOD BOOK GUIDE

⌄ **8-Session Bible Study**

John 1-12 For You

These studies are adapted from *John 1–12 For You*. If you are reading *John 1–12 For You* alongside this Good Book Guide, here is how the studies in this booklet link to the chapters of *John 1–12 For You*:

Study 1 > Ch 1-2

Study 2 > Ch 3

Study 3 > Ch 4-5

Study 4 > Ch 6-7

Study 5 > Ch 8

Study 6 > Ch 9

Study 7 > Ch 10

Study 8 > Ch 11-12

Find out more about *John 1–12 For You* at:
www.thegoodbook.com/for-you

John 1–12: Life to the Full
A Good Book Guide
© Josh Moody/The Good Book Company, 2017.
This edition printed 2025.

Published by The Good Book Company

thegoodbook.com | thegoodbook.co.uk
thegoodbook.com.au | thegoodbook.co.nz | thegoodbook.co.in

thegoodbook
COMPANY

A CIP catalogue record for this book is available from the British Library.

Design by André Parker and Drew McCall

ISBN: 9781802541748 | JOB-008035 | Printed in India

Contents

Introduction

One of the Bible writers described God's word as "a lamp for my feet, a light on my path" (Psalm 119:105, NIV). God gave us the Bible to tell us about who he is and what he wants for us. He speaks through it by his Spirit and lights our way through life.

That means that we need to look carefully at the Bible and uncover its meaning—but we also need to apply what we've discovered to our lives.

Good Book Guides are designed to help you do just that. The sessions in this book are interactive and easy to lead. They're perfect for use in groups or for personal study.

Let's take a look at what is included in each session.

Talkabout: Every session starts with an ice-breaker question, designed to get people talking around a subject that links to the Bible study.

Investigate: These questions help you explore what the passage is about.

Apply: These questions are designed to get you thinking practically: what does this Bible teaching mean for you and your church?

Explore More: These optional sections help you to go deeper or to explore another part of the Bible which connects with the main passage.

Getting Personal: These sections are a chance for personal reflection. Some groups may feel comfortable discussing these, but you may prefer to look at them quietly as individuals instead—or leave them out.

Pray: Here, you're invited to pray in the light of the truths and challenges you've seen in the study.

Each session is also designed to be easily split into two! Watch out for the **Apply** section that comes halfway through, and stop there if you haven't got time to do the whole thing in one go.

In the back of the book, you'll find a **Leader's Guide**, which provides helpful notes on every question, along with everything else that group leaders need in order to facilitate a great session and help the group uncover the riches of God's light-giving word.

Why Study John 1 – 12?

John's Gospel is an invitation to you to find life.

The standard view of the structure of John's Gospel sees John 20:30-31 as the apostle John's definitive statement as to his purpose for writing this book:

> "Jesus performed many other signs in the presence of the disciples, which are not recorded in this book. But these are written that you may believe that Jesus is the Messiah, the Son of God, and that by believing you may have life in his name."

The "signs" that we will see in this Good Book Guide are for a particular purpose: that we may "believe that Jesus is the Messiah, the Son of God, and that by believing [we] may have life in his name."

The key word in some ways is not so much "believe" but "life." John's Gospel is about showing us how to have "life … to the full" (10:10)—fullness of life or life in abundance—in Jesus' name. The discourse with the woman at the well in John chapter 4 illustrates this theme, as Jesus promises her that…

> "whoever drinks the water I give them will never thirst. Indeed, the water I give them will become in them a spring of water welling up to eternal life." (4:13-14)

The eight studies in this Good Book Guide will, I pray, not simply give you a deeper understanding of the text, nor a list of practical to-do's by way of application; rather, I hope they will enable you to encounter more and more deeply Jesus the Messiah, the Son of God. It is as you do so that you will find in him *life*—in all the ramifications that John's Gospel intends.

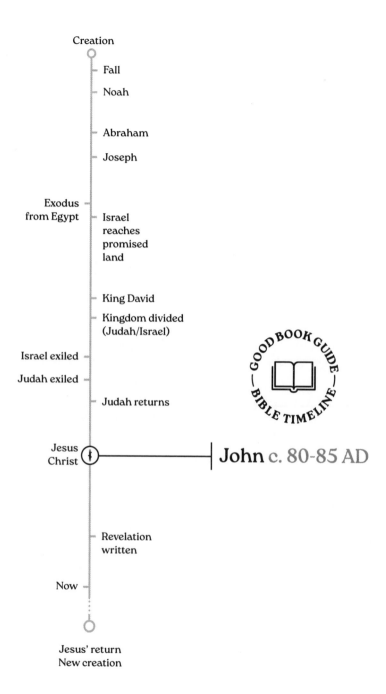

Creation

Fall

Noah

Abraham

Joseph

Exodus
from Egypt

Israel
reaches
promised
land

King David

Kingdom divided
(Judah/Israel)

Israel exiled

Judah exiled

Judah returns

GOOD BOOK GUIDE
BIBLE TIMELINE

Jesus
Christ

John c. 80-85 AD

Revelation
written

Now

Jesus' return
New creation

Meeting the Word

John 1:1 - 2:12

Talkabout

1. If you asked 100 people on the street, "Why did Jesus come to earth 2,000 years ago?", what kinds of answers would you get?

• What about if you asked the same question of people in your church?

Investigate

📖 **Read John 20:30-31**

DICTIONARY

Signs (v 30): miracles.
Messiah (v 31): the all-powerful,

eternal King promised throughout the Old Testament.

---

2. Why did John write his Gospel?

- Read 4:13-14; 10:10. What is the "eternal life" like that belief in Jesus offers?

📖 **Read John 1:1-18**

DICTIONARY

The Word (v 1): God the Son, Jesus Christ.
His own (v 11): the Jewish people.

Glory (v 14): God's awesome presence.

---

3. What do we learn about the Word?

- What is the Word's relationship with God?

Getting Personal | OPTIONAL

Which single verse from this section will you memorize and call to mind throughout each day to remind you of who God is and who you are?

📖 **Read John 1:19-36**

DICTIONARY

Testimony (v 19): evidence.
Elijah (v 21): an important Old
Testament prophet.

The Prophet (v 21): In the Old
Testament God promised to raise up
a prophet greater than Moses (see
Deuteronomy 18:15; Hebrews 3:5-6).

---

4. What does John (not the Gospel writer!), who "came as a witness" (v 7), tell us about Jesus in these verses?

- How does John show remarkable humility in this section?

Apply

5. How do you think these verses should make us feel about Jesus Christ?

6. John's message can be summed up as *Not me but him*. What would it look like for us to live that way in our lives?

Investigate

📖 **Read John 1:37-51**

7. Who do Andrew and Philip realize Jesus is?

8. What is one of the first things that they both do next?

Getting Personal | OPTIONAL

Andrew is less well known to posterity than Simon (or, as he is usually called, Peter), but without Andrew's ministry of bringing, there would not have been Peter's ministry of preaching. If we do not have Andrews, then, under God's providence, we are unlikely to have Peters. You may not be a Peter, but you can be an Andrew.

How might you invite someone to come and see Jesus this week?

---

9. What does Jesus promise Nathanael (v 50-51)?

Explore More | OPTIONAL

📖 Read Genesis 28:10-17

- What did Jacob (who was later renamed Israel, 35:10) see in his dream (28:12)?
- What did he realize was the significance of the dream (v 16-17)?

📖 Reread John 1:51

- According to Jesus, where is this place where heaven touches earth—where we find a stairway to heaven?

📖 Read John 2:1-12

10. What is the purpose of Jesus' miracle here (v 11)?

- What is the right response to it?

11. What do you think the choice of event and the type and amount of wine produced are meant to tell us about Jesus and life with him?

Apply

12. If someone researching Jesus Christ spent a week looking at your life, would they get a picture of the one you follow that is similar to the picture of Jesus that John has given us here?

- How can we use the truths of 1:1 – 2:12 to change our lives in order to reflect better the light that gives life?

Pray

Thank God…

- *that the Word became flesh.*

- *that the Word became flesh so that you could know the Father.*

- *that the Word became flesh to bring life in abundance.*

Ask God…

- *to enable you to live with a "Not me but him" attitude.*

- *to fill you with awe and excitement as you read about the Word in John's Gospel.*

- *to give you a deep and joyful confidence in the power and goodness of the one who turns water into wine.*

2

Out of the Temple, into the Kingdom

John 2:13 – 3:21

The Story So Far...

The Word became flesh to reveal God and give life with God. John the Baptist witnessed to the Word, who revealed his glory by turning water into wine.

Talkabout

1. "Jesus was a great and respected religious leader." Discuss.

Investigate

📖 **Read John 2:12-25**

DICTIONARY

Passover (v 13): festival remembering God's rescue of the Israelites from slavery in Egypt (described in Exodus).

Zeal (v 17): passion.

---

2. What do the events of verses 13-16 show that Jesus hates?

• What does Jesus passionately desire (v 17—see also Mark 11:17)?

3. Why is the question asked by "the Jews" (that is, the leaders of the Jewish religion) a fair one (John 2:18)?

• What will be the evidence that Jesus has the authority to dictate matters in the temple (v 19-21)?

In response, "many ... believed" (v 23). But Jesus "would not entrust himself to them" (v 24). Why not? Because, as the rest of the Gospel will show, people will misinterpret what he is doing and either oppose him, perhaps violently, or take him and try to make him a king or leader who fits their agendas, perhaps again violently.

Apply

The temple was the place where people could access the presence of God. It was the house of God, where God was at home. In verse 19, Jesus says the Old Testament temple building was always about and pointing to him.

4. How can Christians today forget this and so treat other places or people as the "temple"?

5. What should make you angry? Does it?

Getting Personal | OPTIONAL

The sad truth is that we sometimes make it harder for people to find God, not easier, by turning our "temples" of worship into places that make it tough to have access to God. The point of the temple was to be the place where all people could go to meet with God. The same, in that regard at least, is true for church today.

Are you, or your church, raising hurdles that you expect newcomers to clamber over? Are there barriers to people being part of your church, other than the message of the gospel?

Investigate

While Jesus would not "entrust himself" to people, the word about Jesus was getting out to people—and some wanted to find out more. One of those with questions was a member of the religious elite...

📖 **Read John 3:1-21**

DICTIONARY

Pharisee (v 1): religious leaders who took obeying the law, and additional rules, extremely seriously.

The kingdom of God (v 3): God's spiritual kingdom is made up of those people who submit to Christ as their King.

---

6. Why do you think Nicodemus comes to see Jesus in the darkness of night?

7. What does Jesus want Nicodemus to understand (v 3, 5-8)?

8. What is the way to be "born again" into "eternal life" (v 14-16)?

Explore More | OPTIONAL

In verses 14-15, Jesus is referring to an incident that would have been famous in his day, which had taken place when God's people were in the wilderness, with Moses leading them from Egypt to the promised land.

📖 **Read Numbers 21:4-9**

- Why did the people face death by snake?
- What was the only way to escape that death?
- So what is Jesus saying about his death on the cross when he says in John 3 that he will be lifted up in the same way that the bronze snake was in the wilderness?

---

9. How would John 3:17-21 have been both an invitation and a warning to Nicodemus, sitting in the darkness, listening to Jesus?

10. Read 7:50-52 and 19:38-42. What effect does his nighttime conversation with Jesus appear to have had on this great, respected religious leader?

Getting Personal | OPTIONAL

How have you experienced loving darkness in your own life or seen it in someone else's? How have you experienced Jesus' light shining into your darkness?

Is there a way you need to allow Jesus' light to shine into an area of your life today, and to change as you come into his light?

Apply

11. If someone asked you, "What does it mean to be born again?", what would you say, from this passage?

12. What was Jesus' relationship with religion? How is this both liberating for us and a warning to us, in our religious lives today?

Pray

Praise God...

- *that his Son is so passionate about people having access to him.*

- *that, in Jesus, you come to the true temple and can meet with him.*

- *for giving you new birth, and all which that means.*

Ask God...

- *for the same zeal for bringing people to come to know God that Jesus had.*

- *to give you confidence that the Spirit must, and can, bring new birth to anyone, and can cause you to speak confidently of how the Son of Man was lifted up.*

3

Strange Harvest and Religious Red Tape

John 3:22 - 5:18

The Story So Far...

The Word became flesh to reveal God and give life with God. John the Baptist witnessed to the Word, who revealed his glory by turning water to wine.

Jesus was so angered by religion that blocks access to God that he cleared the temple. Even a religious leader must be "born again" to enter God's kingdom.

Talkabout

1. When are religious rules a good thing? Are they ever a bad thing, and if so, why?

Investigate

📖 **Read John 3:22-36**

DICTIONARY

Wrath (v 36): God's right, settled anger against sin.

2. Why do John's disciples appear to be jealous (v 22-26)?

3. How does John's response...
  • showcase Christian humility?

  • show us how we can be effective witnesses to Christ?

📖 **Read John 4:1-42**

4. Where is Jesus, and who does he speak with (v 4-8)?

5. What does Jesus...
  • offer this woman?

  • tell this woman?

- Why does she, and the townspeople, end up believing that "this man really is the Savior of the world" (v 25-26, 39-42)?

Getting Personal | OPTIONAL

Do you experience this "living water"? This is not mechanical engagement with religion or church, but a personal relationship with Jesus.

Is this your experience of God? Would you ask Jesus to give you increasingly his living water—his Spirit?

---

6. What does Jesus say has been going on at this well (v 35-38)?

Apply

7. How can focusing too much on ourselves...
   - stop us witnessing?

   - cause us to witness in an ineffective way?

8. Who are the people in your area who would be the strangest gospel harvest, as this much-married Samaritan woman was here? How can you initiate conversations with them, and how can you communicate the gospel to them?

Investigate

📖 **Read John 4:43-54**

9. What does this second "sign" tell us about Jesus?

Getting Personal | OPTIONAL

Jesus does not have to be next to us in body for his word to have its powerful healing, saving, encouraging impact, for he is next to us by his Spirit.

In what circumstances in your own life do you find it hard to believe God could be at work? How will you use this story to encourage yourself?

📖 **Read John 5:1-18**

10. Why do Jesus' actions and words cause such trouble (v 8-10, 16-18)?

11. In what sense are the Jewish leaders correct? In what way are they making a mistake?

Explore More | OPTIONAL

- What does Jesus suggest about this man's suffering and his sin in verse 14?
- What else does Jesus say about the link between suffering and sin in 9:1-3?
- How should we therefore respond to suffering in our lives?

Apply

It is easier than any of us will want to admit to refashion biblical obedience into restrictive human-centered tokens of pride and communal distinction, as the religious leaders had done with the Sabbath.

12. Is your church culture in any danger of elevating particular rules—perhaps made for very good reasons—above loving and serving Jesus?

- What will you do about this?

Pray

Use your answers to the Getting Personal section on page 22, and your answers to question 12, to shape your prayers.

4

Food That Will Not Spoil

John 5:17 - 6:71

The Story So Far...

The Word became flesh to reveal God and give life with God. John the Baptist witnessed to the Word, who revealed his glory by turning water to wine.

Jesus was so angered by religion that blocks access to God that he cleared the temple. Even a religious leader must be "born again" to enter his kingdom.

Jesus, the one who is equal with God because he is God, offered "living water." Outsiders loved him, but the religious elite were angered by him.

Talkabout

1. What do we need in order to feel satisfied in life?

Investigate

📖 **Read John 5:17-30**

DICTIONARY

Sabbath (v 18): Jewish holy day; God commanded his people to do no work on the Sabbath.

Imagine what it must have been like for a 1st-century Jew, part of the most vigorously monotheistic people the world had ever seen, to process the claim that a person standing in front of them was equal to God the Father. But this was exactly what Jesus was claiming in verse 18. These verses are Jesus' answer to the charge that his claim to be God is blasphemous because it is false (see verse 19). This is Jesus' answer to the question: are you really God?

2. What does Jesus claim in verses 19-29, and how do those claims back up his argument that he is equal to God the Father?
- v 19, 30

- v 20a

- v 20b

- v 21

- v 22

- v 23

- v 24-25

- v 26

- v 27-29

Next, Jesus calls four "witnesses" to back up his claim to divinity.

📖 **Read John 5:31-47**

3. Who are those witnesses, and how do they support him?
- v 32-35

- v 36

- v 37-40

- v 45-47

Getting Personal | OPTIONAL

When you strip away the complexity of different approaches to the Scriptures, there is a basic affectional orientation, a heart love, which either allows us to encounter Jesus in the Scriptures or prevents us from doing so. The question is not *Do we read the Scriptures carefully?* but rather *Do we have the love of God within us?*

Do you study the Scriptures? And do you do so out of love for God and a desire to see Jesus there?

Explore More | OPTIONAL

📖 **Read Deuteronomy 18:15**

- How did Moses testify about Jesus?

So we need to ask: what is it that makes Jesus a prophet like Moses?

📖 **Read Exodus 3:7-10**

- What did God do for his people through Moses?
- What can we expect God to do for his people through Jesus?

📖 **Read John 6:1-15**

4. What does Jesus provide for the people, and how?

5. What is he showing about himself, do the crowd realize (v 14)?

- Read Exodus 16:1-16. How is Jesus re-enacting this event from Israel's time in the wilderness?

But the crowd are only half-right. Jesus realizes that they have gone from viewing him as an all-in-one free healthcare solution (John 6:2) to an aggressive military ruler about to throw out the Romans and re-establish the Davidic kingdom (v 15)—from one extreme to another.

But if he has not come to be either of those things… who is he?

📖 **Read John 6:16-21 and Exodus 3:7-14**

6. "It is I" (John 6:20) is the Greek translation of the Hebrew "I am." What is Jesus claiming in verse 20?

• How does where he is standing add credibility to his claim?!

Apply

7. What would the crowd's two misunderstandings of the nature of Jesus' kingship—a healthcare service or an aggressive political/military leader—look like in your society or church?

Investigate

We come now to one of the more lengthy discourses in the Gospel. Contained in it are various puzzles of some complexity, but basically the whole discussion is framed by Jesus' feeding of the five thousand. This marks Jesus out as a prophet at least on equal terms with Moses, through whom God provided manna to his people in Old Testament Israel, but Jesus wants to take the discussion several steps further. He is not just offering "bread"; he is offering "the bread of life." What does that mean?

📖 **Read John 6:22-71**

8. According to Jesus, what are the crowds looking for from him (v 26)? What is the problem with what they are seeking?

Instead, he says, they need to find "food that endures to eternal life." Jesus does not just give this bread (v 27); he is this bread (v 35).

9. What is true of anyone who eats the bread of life (v 35, 48-51, 53-58)?

- How does a person "eat" this "bread" (v 40)?

- What makes a person able to eat the "bread" (v 37, 39-40, 44, 65)?

- How is this humbling and reassuring?

10. How does the crowd respond?
   - v 41-42

   - v 52

   - v 60

   - v 66

- Why is Jesus' teaching here so "hard," do you think?

11. Why does Peter not join those who are walking away from following Jesus?

Apply

12. In what ways do we work for food that spoils? What does it look like to feed on the bread of life instead?

Getting Personal | OPTIONAL

Feed on Jesus and you will never hunger; you will always be fully and eternally satisfied. When this week will you most need to remember this?

Pray

"I am the bread of life. Whoever comes to me will never go hungry."

(John 6:35)

Use this verse to prompt your praise and prayers.

5

Dividing Lines and Drawing in the Dust

John 7:1 - 8:30

The Story So Far...

Jesus was so angered by religion that blocks access to God that he cleared the temple. Even a religious leader must be "born again" to enter God's kingdom.

Jesus, the one who is equal with God because he is God, offered "living water." Outsiders loved him. But the religious elite were angered by him.

Jesus fed thousands with miraculous bread and walked on water to show that he is God, and that he is eternal "living bread" for those who believe in him.

Talkabout

1. Who are the most divisive public figures in your culture or country? What makes them so divisive?

Investigate

📖 **Read John 7:1-11**

2. Why does Jesus not want to travel around Judea (v 1)?

- What do Jesus' brothers want him to do (v 2-4)? Why (v 5)?

Then Jesus says he will not go (v 8), before going (v 10)! Jesus meant that he was not going up to this festival at the same time as his brothers were going, because his time—the moment when he would receive due attention and show himself to the world—had not yet fully come.

📖 **Read John 7:12-52**

3. What opinions about Jesus are on display here, and who holds each?
   - v 12a

- v 12b

- v 15

- v 20

- v 25-27

- v 31, 40-41

- v 41-42

- v 46

The Festival of Tabernacles was one of the great annual feasts given in the Old Testament. Moses commanded God's people that they should "live in temporary shelters for seven days" (Leviticus 23:42), because in so doing, they were reminding themselves of God's rescue of them from Egypt.

Additionally, it is probable that there was an especial emphasis upon water. A water libation—that is, a pouring out of water—was performed at the temple. As the water was poured out, it is likely they would have recited Psalm 118, regarded as a messianic psalm: "LORD, save us! LORD, grant us success! Blessed is he who comes in the name of the LORD. From the house of the LORD we bless you" (Psalm 118:25-26).

4. How does this heighten the drama of what Jesus cries out in John 7:37-38?

- What does he mean by this (v 39)?

Getting Personal | OPTIONAL

The 19th-century preacher C.H. Spurgeon once said, "To the unbeliever, Christ is nothing. But to the believer, Christ is everything. To the unbeliever, a mere opinion about Christ is everything. To the true believer, the saving knowledge of Christ has covered up all mere opinions concerning Him. He knows Christ, and lives in Him, and Christ also lives in him."

What is Christ to you?

Apply

5. What do you think it means to experience the Spirit's streams of living water flowing within you?

- What difference does believing in Jesus, rather than dismissing him in one way or another, make in daily life?

Investigate

The textual location of the episode at the start of chapter 8 has long been doubted. This is not the place to rehearse the arguments. Suffice it to say that even if this account is not originally a part of this narrative, it certainly fits well, and seems to me to have definitely been authentic to Christ, whether or not it was originally located here or elsewhere in the Gospels.

📖 **Read John 8:1-11**

6. By the end of verse 5, what two options does it seem Jesus must choose between?

- How would either choice spring the "trap" the religious leaders have set (v 6)? What would each choice allow them to accuse Jesus of?

Explore More | OPTIONAL

A good question to ask is whether the religious leaders are right: did Moses command God's people to "stone such women"?

📖 **Read Leviticus 20:10**

- If the religious leaders in John 8 had truly cared about Mosaic justice, who else would have been standing before Jesus?

📖 **Scan-read Leviticus 1:1-9; 2 Samuel 11:1-5; Psalm 51**

- What did the Old Testament law provide for those who had done something worthy of death, such as committing adultery?

---

7. How do Jesus' words and actions neither condemn the woman nor condone her sin?

8. In what sense does every human stand where that woman stood?

📖 **Read John 8:12-30**

9. What is wonderful about the image of himself that the Lord gives us in verse 12?

- What excuse do the Pharisees come up with for rejecting his claim (v 13)?

10. At what point will there be no doubt about whether Jesus is who he claims to be (v 28-29)?

- Read Acts 2:32-41. How do we see Jesus' words in John 7:28-29 coming true here?

Getting Personal | OPTIONAL

How will you look to Jesus as your guiding light today, in a way that you did not, or struggled to, yesterday?

How do you need Jesus to tell you today, "Go, and leave your life of sin"?

Apply

11. How does Jesus guide us here to have a high view of sin, and an even higher view of grace? Which do you find it harder to have a high enough view of?

- How would this apply to, for example, a member of your church who has committed adultery?

12. How does identifying ourselves with the woman stop us from acting like the Pharisees? How does it cause us to love Jesus more?

Pray

Share what has most excited you and challenged you from this passage (be specific), and then pray for each other.

6

Free to See the Light

John 8:31 - 9:41

The Story So Far...

Jesus, the one who is equal with God because he is God, offered "living water." Outsiders loved him. But the religious elite were angered by him.

Jesus fed thousands with miraculous bread and walked on water to show that he is God, and that he is eternal "living bread" for those who believe in him.

People were divided over Jesus' identity—but those who believed in him as King enjoyed his Spirit in them, his forgiveness from him, and his light to guide them.

Talkabout

1. What does it mean to be free? Why is freedom so important to us?

Investigate

📖 **Read John 8:31-47**

DICTIONARY

Abraham (v 33): Israel's "founding father." God promised to bless Abraham and make his descendants into a great nation.

2. Look at what Jesus says about the route to real freedom (v 31-32). What is strange about it?

3. What does Jesus say that all people need to be freed from, and for (v 34-36)?

4. Why does this language of slavery and freedom offend those who are listening to him (v 33)?

• How does Jesus answer their claim that they do not need to be set free because they are not slaves, but rather, children of Abraham (v 39-47)?

📖 **Read John 8:48-59**

5. What is Jesus' relationship to Abraham?

• How could Abraham have seen Jesus, when Jesus is less than 50 years old (v 57)?

Explore More | OPTIONAL

"Abraham rejoiced at the thought of seeing my day." The following passages help us understand what Jesus means here.

📖 **Read Genesis 18:16-33; 22:1-19**

- When Abraham "saw the LORD" or saw "the angel of the LORD," who does he seem to have been seeing?

📖 **Read Hebrews 11:8-19**

- What was Abraham gladly looking forward to?

Getting Personal | OPTIONAL

Ask yourself whether your life is being lived for Jesus, or for yourself. Are you acting as if there is a more important truth than this one, and a way to be set free other than this one?

Apply

Jesus' teaching—the teaching of the Scriptures—is "the perfect law that gives freedom" (James 1:25).

6. When do you find it hardest to believe this? Why?

7. Why is knowing "the truth [that] will set you free" good news for a relativistic society, where everyone's truth is seen as equally valid?

Investigate

Now, in this story that is all about sight and blindness, we continue to discover who is free, and who is in the dark.

📖 **Read John 9:1-7**

8. Who comes from blindness to sight, and how?

📖 **Read John 9:8-41**

DICTIONARY

Put out of the synagogue
(v 22): banned from the local place
of worship.

9. What does Jesus accuse the Pharisees of (v 40-41)?

- How have the Pharisees already shown the truth of Jesus' accusation (v 13-34)?

10. What does spiritual sight look like (v 35-38)?

Apply

Once again, it is the religiously well-informed who see a miracle performed by Jesus himself but refuse to see what is in front of them.

11. How do we spot if we are in danger of the spiritual pride that can blind us to truly seeing, and experiencing, God?

12. Is it possible to overvalue intellectual capacity and knowing the Bible? What might this look like in your church?

Getting Personal | OPTIONAL

We need, then, whoever we are, to defeat our religious pride. We do that if and as we have a personal encounter with Christ, recognizing him for who he is and allowing him to show us where we are mistaken, so that we experience with him an ongoing life of joyful, though costly, discipleship.

How has that happened, and how is that happening, in your own life?

When was the last time you let Jesus show you that you were wrong in some way?

When was the last time you simply told Jesus, "Lord, I believe you are the Son of Man" and worshiped him?

Pray

Share ways that you have experienced the freedom of obeying Jesus, and thank him for giving you eyes to see what will truly set you free.

Share specific ways you find it hard to believe that obedience will free you, and spend some time praying for one another.

Finish by using the truth of these words to praise Jesus: "Very truly I tell you ... before Abraham was born, I am!" (John 8:58)

7

The Controversial Shepherd

John 10:1-42

The Story So Far...

Jesus fed thousands with miraculous bread and walked on water to show that he is God, and that he is eternal "living bread" for those who believe in him.

People were divided over Jesus' identity—but those who believed in him as King enjoyed his Spirit in them, his forgiveness from him, and his light to guide them.

Obeying Jesus' truth leads to true freedom. Jesus healed a man born blind, and the leaders' reaction to the healing showed that they were spiritually blind.

Talkabout

1. What makes someone a good shepherd?

- How would you sum up what sheep are like, in three words?

Investigate

The way shepherding was (and is still) done in the Middle East was different from the techniques in Western countries like Britain or Australia:

"Unlike Western shepherds who drive the sheep, often using a sheep dog, the shepherds of the Near East, both now and in Jesus' day, lead their flock, their voice calling them on. That such a shepherd goes ahead of his sheep and draws them constitutes an admirable picture of the master/disciple relationship. The sheep follow simply because they know his voice; by the same token, they will run from anyone else because they do not recognize a stranger's voice." (D.A. Carson, *John*, p. 383)

📖 **Read John 10:1-21**

DICTIONARY

Sheepfold/sheep pen (v 1):
enclosure where several different shepherds' flocks were kept at night.

---

2. What kinds of people enter sheep pens, and how do the sheep respond differently to those people (v 1-5)?

• Who do you think each person represents?

Now Jesus switches metaphors in a way that would probably frustrate early-education teachers the world over. Jesus is not only the shepherd; he is also "the gate" (v 7)!

3. What does Jesus promise to sheep who enter "through me" (v 7-10)?

4. In what ways is Jesus a "good" shepherd (v 11-18)?

• What characterizes Jesus' sheep (v 11-18)?

Apply

5. What is both humbling and wonderful about being a sheep of the good shepherd? In what situations will this be particularly comforting?

Getting Personal | OPTIONAL

No one who follows this good shepherd, who gives up his life for the sheep, can expect an easy life. But everyone who does so is promised a full life. Better fully to live even at great cost than never to truly live at all.

How are you enjoying life in all its fullness by following your shepherd's voice? Are there ways in which you are wandering and need to return?

---

6. How do we, as Jesus' sheep, hear his voice?

Investigate

📖 **Read John 10:22-42**

7. Where is Jesus now in these verses, and what is he there for (v 22-23)?

So the question is: *who will commit themselves to Jesus?*

8. Why can't the religious leaders realize that Jesus is the Messiah (v 25-26)?

9. What does Jesus promise about his sheep (v 28-30)?

Getting Personal | OPTIONAL

"I give them eternal life, and they shall never perish; no one will snatch them out of my hand" (v 28).

How will you memorize this wonderful verse? When do you most need to remember it?

Explore More | OPTIONAL

Jesus' claim in verse 30—"I and the Father are one"—prompts the Jewish opponents to scour around for stones to kill him for his blasphemy (v 33).

- How does Jesus answer the charge (v 34-36)?

📖 **Read Psalm 82**

- Who are the "gods" of verse 6?
- Why will they "fall like every other ruler" (v 2, 5)?

Israel's teachers had such special spiritual advantages that they were like "gods"—yet they acted and behaved just like the rest of the world, and would be held accountable (v 1, 5).

- Why should Jesus, who is claiming something even greater, be believed (John 10:37-38)?

---

10. Where does Jesus find his sheep (v 40-42)?

"Across the Jordan," away from the elite "gods" of the temple (see Explore More above) and the special religious festival, is where people come to believe in him (v 42). The truth is that, if we are not very careful, familiarity breeds contempt.

Apply

11. During which religious festival, or season of the year, do you find it easiest to forget about Jesus and fail to worship him?

- What can you do to change how you walk through that time as a sheep of Jesus?

12. What has particularly struck you about the nature and work of our good shepherd?

Pray

Use your answers to question 12 to thank Jesus for being your good shepherd.

Then use your answers to questions 5 and 11 to ask Jesus to help you listen to his voice and follow him. Share a particular situation, time, or need in which you particularly require the comfort or guidance or protection of your good shepherd this week, and pray about that.

8

The Resurrection and the Life

John 11:1 - 12:50

The Story So Far...

People were divided over Jesus' identity—but those who believed in him as King enjoyed his Spirit in them, his forgiveness from him, and his light to guide them.

Obeying Jesus' truth leads to true freedom. Jesus healed a man born blind, and the leaders' reaction to the healing showed that they were spiritually blind.

Jesus is the good shepherd, who lays down his life for his sheep and leads them into abundant life. His sheep are those who listen to and follow him.

Talkabout

1. What phrases or euphemisms does your society use for death?

- Why do you think we are often so keen to avoid simply saying, "They died and were buried"?

Investigate

📖 **Read John 11:1-16**

2. What is strange about Jesus' response to hearing that his friend Lazarus is gravely ill (v 5-6)?

• How do verses 4 and 11-15 explain his delay?

• What are we being told about delayed answers to desperate prayers?

Getting Personal | OPTIONAL

It is a strange thought that the Lord's love sometimes means delayed answers to the most urgent of requests. But that was the experience of Lazarus and his sisters—and it's the common experience of Christians today.

Do you need to hear this today? Are there ways in which you've concluded that delays are down to a lack of care for you?

Who do you know today who needs to hear and believe the truth about the Lord's love in delays?

📖 **Read John 11:17-45**

DICTIONARY

The last day (v 24): the day in the future when God will raise the dead for judgment.

Strips of linen (v 44): cloth used to wrap bodies before burial.

3. What is comforting for the Christian in…
   • v 25-26?

   • v 33-35?

   • v 43-44?

📖 **Read John 11:46 – 12:11**

4. What reactions to Jesus do we see encapsulated by the following people? What motivates each reaction?
   • Caiaphas (11:47-50)

   • Mary (12:1-3)

   • Judas (v 4-6)

5. What is tragic, and ironic, about the leaders' reaction to "the resurrection and the life" bringing a dead man back to life (11:53; 12:10-11)?

Apply

6. What would it look like for you to live as Mary did? (Be specific.)

- How does John 11 motivate you to live this way?

Investigate

📖 **Read John 12:12-50**

DICTIONARY

Hosanna (v 13): a word meaning something like "Salvation is here!"
Blessed (v 13): favored by God.
Daughter Zion (v 15): a name for

Israel (Zion was the mountain on which Jerusalem was built).
The prince of this world (v 31): the devil.

---

7. What does it tell us about Jesus that he chose to enter Jerusalem on a young donkey (v 14-15—read Zechariah 9:9-10)?

8. What responses to this humble King do we see (John 12:17-22)?

9. Read 7:30 and 8:20. What is hugely significant about 12:23?

- What does the arrival of Jesus' hour mean for him (v 24-33)?

Explore More | OPTIONAL

- How did the people who had seen "so many signs" respond (v 37)?

This unbelief is a specific fulfillment of a prophetic prediction.

📖 **Read Isaiah 6:8-13 and 53:1-3**

- Why do people not believe the words of the prophets, such as Isaiah 6:8-13?
- Who is responsible for the blindness?
- What does this tell us about what humans are naturally like?
- In light of this, how would people view the Lord's servant (53:1-3)?
- How have we seen this fulfilled in Jesus' ministry in the first twelve chapters of John's Gospel?

---

10. What does Jesus say life will be like for his followers (John 12:25-26)?

- How does this reveal the inadequate nature of the "belief" we see in verses 42-43?

Getting Personal | OPTIONAL

Whatever stage of the Christian life we are at, we must beware, lest we fall into the same trap. Whose glory is it that we seek? That of people—or that of the Other? The glory and approval of people is far less satisfying than the all-surpassing glory of the Eternal One. To hear one word of praise from him is worth more than a lifetime of approval from this world.

Does this liberate you or challenge you, personally? How?

---

11. What does Jesus remind the people about regarding the purpose of his coming (v 44-47)?

- But what warning does he also give (v 48)?

Apply

12. How would you use the first twelve chapters of John's Gospel to explain…
    - who Jesus is? (Think of his teaching, but also of the images he has used.)

- what the life he offers is like?

- what true, life-to-the-full-bringing belief is like?

Pray

Use your answers to question 12 to fuel your prayers of thanksgiving, and your answers to question 6 to fuel your prayers of petition.

Share your favorite verse from John 1 – 12 with the group, and then use this collection of verses to finish by praising Jesus for all he is, and all he has done and is doing for you.

John 1–12

Life to the Full

Leader's Guide: Introduction

This Leader's Guide includes guidance for every question. It will provide background information and help you if you get stuck. For each session, you'll also find the following:

The Big Idea: The main point of the session, in brief. This is what you should be aiming to have fixed in people's minds by the end of the session!

Summary: An overview of the passage you're reading together.

Optional Extra: Usually this is an introductory activity that ties in with the main theme of the Bible study and is designed to break the ice at the beginning of a session. Or it may be a "homework project" that people can tackle during the week.

Occasionally the Leader's Guide includes an extra follow-up question, printed in *italics*. This doesn't appear in the main study guide but could be a useful add-on to help your group get to the answer or go deeper.

Here are a few key principles to bear in mind as you prepare to lead:

- Don't just read out the answers from the Leader's Guide. Ideally, you want the group to discover these answers from the Bible for themselves.

- Keep drawing people back to the passage you're studying. People may come up with answers based on their experiences or on teaching they've heard in the past, but the point of this study is to listen to God's word itself—so keep directing your group to look at the text.

- Make sure everyone finishes the session knowing how the passage is relevant for them. We do Bible study so that our lives can be changed by what we hear from God's word. So, **Apply** questions aren't just an add-on—they're a vital part of the session.

Finally, remember that your group is unique! You should feel free to use this Good Book Guide in a way that works for them. If they're a quiet bunch, you might want to spend longer on the **Talkabout** question. If they love to get creative, try using mind-mapping or doodling to kick-start some of your discussions. If your time is limited, you can choose to skip **Explore More** or split the whole session into two. Adapt the material in whatever way you think will help your group get the most out of God's word.

1

Meeting the Word

John 1:1 - 2:12

The Big Idea

The eternal, divine Word came to earth in the person of Jesus the Messiah to bring abundant, joyful, eternal, heavenly life to people like us.

Summary

John's "prologue" is one of the most profound parts of John, but at the same time its message is quite simple. Probably the easiest way to understand its main theme is by comparing the beginning and end of this introduction to John's Gospel (v 1, 18). John introduces us to the Word, and then tells us that the Word became flesh (v 14) so that the Father would be made known by his Son (v 18). The underpinning "logos," or structure and order of the universe, is all centered on a person.

These verses also introduce the role of John the Baptist. He is the witness to the Word, and his role is further developed from verse 19. He humbly points away from himself and toward Jesus, saying in effect, *Not me but him* (v 19-36). Accordingly, John's disciples are among those who begin to follow Jesus, the Messiah, who is the place where heaven touches earth (v 37-51).

This study finishes with Jesus' first sign, in which he turns water to wine, revealing his glory (2:1-12)—which *both* demonstrates that his rule is one of feasting

and fullness *and* calls for the response of belief in him (v 11).

Optional Extra

Jesus' kingdom is one of feasting and fullness! So start or finish your session together by sharing some special food or drink.

Guidance for Questions

1. **If you asked 100 people on the street, "Why did Jesus come to earth 2,000 years ago?", what kinds of answers would you get?**
There will be many answers, some more accurate than others. Of course, some may question whether Jesus even did exist 2,000 years ago.

- **What about if you asked the same question of people in your church?**
Hopefully, the answers would be different than out on the street. The main answer is likely to be "To die for our sins"—a "John 1:29 shaped" answer. Return to this question after question 2 and/or 3, and/or 11, and ask how John answers this question. Answers now should include "To bring abundant, joy-filled, real life."

2. **Why did John write his Gospel?**
The "signs" that John describes (which are covered in this Good Book

Guide) are for a particular purpose: namely, that we may "believe that Jesus is the Messiah, the Son of God, and that by believing [we] may have life in his name."

- **Read 4:13-14; 10:10. What is the "eternal life" like that belief in Jesus offers?**

  It is to experience something akin to being thirsty and then finding a source of water that means no more thirst, ever. It is not just life forever, but a life of fullness.

3. **What do we learn about the Word?**

   NOTE: The Word's relationship with God is dealt with in the second part of this question.

   - v 1: He is eternal.
   - v 3: This is the Word by which God made everything.
   - v 4-5: The Word gives life to humans.
   - v 5, 9-10: The Word is not understood by the world, but equally the world has not overcome the Word.
   - v 14: The Word became human, so that people could see him.
   - NOTE: Literally, the Word "dwelt" or "tabernacled" among us. God, in the Old Testament, commanded that a tabernacle be put up in the desert as the place where he symbolically dwelt (Exodus 40:34). But now the real and full glory of God dwells with us—"tabernacles" with us—in the very person of the Word become flesh.
   - John 1:16: Through the Word, we can receive "one gracious blessing after another" (NLT).

- v 17: This grace, and the revelation of truth, came through the person Jesus Christ.
- v 18: If we want to know God, we can do so only through the Word/ the Son.

- **What is the Word's relationship with God?**

  - v 1-3: In the beginning the Word existed, both as God and with God. He shares the same essence as God (the Father), though they differ in person. The sense is of an eternal relationship face to face between coequal Persons enjoying relationship with each other.
  - v 14: The Word is God the Son, who came from God the Father.
  - v 18: The Word is the way God the Father makes himself known. If you want to know the Father, you must know the Son.

4. **What does John (not the Gospel writer!), who "came as a witness" (v 7), tell us about Jesus in these verses?**

   - v 26-27: Important as John is as God's prophet, he pales into insignificance compared to the one who is to come, and in fact already is among the people.
   - v 29: Jesus is "the Lamb of God, who takes away the sin of the world." John is saying that all the sacrifice of lambs at the temple—all that memory of the Passover event, when Israel remembered how God had rescued them from Egypt and had passed over them—was now

fulfilled. God had sent his judgment on everyone, and all people, Israelite and Egyptian alike, were liable to that terrible judgment. But those who were covered by the sacrificial lamb—by the blood of that lamb daubed on the door posts—were passed over. There was a sacrifice in their place.

- v 32-34: John had been given a specific divine message: that the Spirit of God would descend from heaven on the Messiah; and this is how John had recognized Jesus as the one who was to come after him. God the Father, Son, and Holy Spirit rejoice together at this moment when their rescue plan for the world, the Word of God made flesh, is recognized by John the Baptist.

- **How does John show remarkable humility in this section?**
So focused was he on who Christ is that he was able to point others to him, making sure that his very own followers understood that the really important person was not himself but Jesus. Despite his popularity and people wondering if he might be the Messiah, God's long-promised King, John is saying, *Not me but him.* A significant part of John's preaching was telling people that he was nothing special.

5. **How do you think these verses should make us feel about Jesus Christ?**
Many things! Awe. Worship. Joy. Gratitude. Excitement.

You might like to pause here to pray—encourage your group members to start their prayer with a sentence from verses 1-34, which they can then use to praise the Word.

○ *OPTIONAL: Do you struggle more to appreciate the all-powerful divinity of God's Son or the humble humanity of God's Son? How have these verses helped you?*

6. **John's message can be summed up as *Not me but him.* What would it look like for us to live that way in our lives?**
It is more often true than we like to admit that all our motives are shockingly mixed—all of which makes John the Baptist's approach to Jesus remarkable. He honestly, humbly wanted Jesus to be exalted even if that meant he was forgotten. He pointed people to Jesus rather than to himself, despite his own popularity. If we would be the same, we must be willing to trade our own reputation or status, both within our church and outside it, for promoting Jesus' glory. And we will see it as the greatest privilege of our lives to point toward him rather than to promote ourselves.

Think about how this might transform your group's thinking about their family, their friendship group, their ministry, or their workplace.

7. **Who do Andrew and Philip realize Jesus is?**
- v 41: The Messiah.
- v 45: The one Moses had spoken of

and about whom the prophets had foretold—that is, the fulfillment of all God's promises through the Old Testament.

8. **What is one of the first things that they both do next?**
They both find someone else (in Andrew's case, his brother Simon—in Philip's, his friend Nathanael) and bring them to meet Jesus. Their instinct upon meeting Jesus and recognizing who he is is to invite others to discover this for themselves.

9. **What does Jesus promise Nathanael (v 50-51)?**
"You will see greater things than that [i.e. Jesus knowing Nathanael was under the fig tree before he even met him]" (v 50)—essentially, *You ain't seen nothing yet*. And he adds that Nathanael "will see 'heaven open, and the angels of God ascending and descending on' the Son of Man" (v 51). For more on this, see Explore More section below—but in summary, Jesus is saying that he himself provides access to God.

Explore More
○ *Read Genesis 28:10-17. What did Jacob (who was later renamed Israel, 35:10) see in his dream (28:12)?*
The angels of God ascending and descending on a ladder.

○ *What did he realize was the significance of the dream (v 16-17)?*
• *v 16: The Lord was there.*
• *v 17: The place where Jacob had*

slept was *"the house of God ["Bethel"] ... the gate of heaven"—that is, the place on earth where heaven could be accessed.*

○ *Reread John 1:51. According to Jesus, where is this place where heaven touches earth—where we find a stairway to heaven?*
Not in a place, but in a person—in him. The "greater things" that Nathanael will see (v 50) are Jesus' death, resurrection, and ascension, as Jesus himself provides the means of access to God. Jesus is the true "Bethel." The true house of God, and the city of God all center upon him.

---

10. **What is the purpose of Jesus' miracle here (2:11)?**
Jesus shows his "glory"—his "Godness" or nature—through this, the first of the seven signs of John's Gospel. In this moment of joy, Jesus' glory is seen.

• **What is the right response to it?**
To believe in him (see 20:30-31 and question 2). When we truly see Jesus for who he truly is—when we grasp his beauty and glory—then we are moved toward faith in and commitment to him.

11. **What do you think the choice of event and the type and amount of wine produced are meant to tell us about Jesus and life with him?**
Throughout the Old Testament, weddings and marriage had been

symbolic of God's relationship with his people. The prophet Hosea especially played off this theme, but its roots are found in Genesis 2. Paul tells us that marriage is a mystery designed by God to show us Christ's love for the church (Ephesians 5:32). Part of what is revealed here, then, is Jesus' special, joyful love for his people at this wedding. Jesus first reveals his glory not at a funeral, not at a business meeting, not at a sport competition, but at a wedding.

It is instructive of who Jesus is that when he turns water into wine, it is not a poor kind, but the best. God's new work in Jesus is going to be centered on celebration, joy, festival, and that sign of the new covenant, wine.

12. If someone researching Jesus Christ spent a week looking at your life, would they get a picture of the one you follow that is similar to the picture of Jesus that John has given us here?

Jesus shows his glory at a massive, long, olden-days party. And not only does he do it at a party, but he does it by producing gallons of wine—so much wine that it would have been impossible to have drunk it all at the party. Whoever this Jesus is, he is not what religion has made him out to be. He brings joy and overflowing provision.

There are certainly many reasons for us to lament, but joy is to be the hallmark of the Christian, because we know the one who turns water

into wine. Challenge your group as to whether a visitor to their homes would witness grudging duty in their Christian lives, joyless cutting of corners and doing the minimum—or a joyful relationship with and belief in Jesus.

- **How can we use the truths of 1:1 – 2:12 to change our lives in order to reflect better the light that gives life?**

Our joyful service of this Jesus will only come as we enjoy the truth of who he is and so live in joyful reliance on him. He is the light who gives us life, and life in all its fullness. So end by asking people in your group each to identify which truth about Jesus they will use this week to help them find joy in their particular circumstances.

2

Out of the Temple, into the Kingdom

John 2:13 – 3:21

The Big Idea

Jesus was angered by false religion that blocked access to God; he came to be lifted up in order to be the way that anyone can be forgiven and enjoy total access to his Father. It is only by the work of the Spirit, and not through our own religious activity, that we can believe in him and find life.

Summary

For many people today, one of the greatest barriers to true faith in God is fake religion. It is possible to have a significant enough exposure to "religion" that it functions as a sort of inoculation against the real thing. For those of us who are "religious," we all too easily default to legalism, to Pharisaism.

And now along comes this section of John to countermand all that. First, Jesus discovers, evidently to his horror, a commercial enterprise in full swing in the temple, and so he drives out of there these people who are making money in the temple (2:13-16). If there is one thing that makes Jesus livid, it is fake religion that blocks access to God. And in response to the religious leaders' objections, Jesus points to himself as the true temple—the ultimate way that God can be accessed (v 19-21). We need to ask

ourselves whether our churches are doing anything that similarly blocks people's access to God by obscuring Jesus.

Next, Jesus meets a confused religious leader: Nicodemus (3:1-2). Jesus tells this respected teacher that he must be born again (v 3), and that this is something that he cannot do himself—it will require the work of the Spirit in him (v 4-8) to enable him to look at Jesus, when Jesus is lifted up on the cross, with the eyes of faith that will see his death as a saving work (v 13-15). Jesus has come to give eternal life to a world that does not want it (v 16-21).

Optional Extra

To introduce the theme of being "born again," ask group members to bring a photo of themselves as a newborn, if they have one. Collect the photos at the start of the session and arrange them on a table. Group members must try and work out who's who. If you have time, ask people to share when and where they were born— and (if appropriate for your group) when and where they were "born again."

Guidance for Questions

1. **"Jesus was a great and respected religious leader." Discuss.**

   There is no right or wrong response to this statement—in many ways, it depends on what we mean by "religious" and whose respect we are referring to. You'll return to discussing this in question 12, in light of the passage being studied. But what is certain is that Jesus' strongest adverse reactions were to religious leaders who were leading people wrongly, and who thought they were doing nothing wrong. He reserves his most acute opposition for Pharisees, not for prostitutes, and for temple religion gone wrong rather than for people who get drunk.

2. **What do the events of verses 13-16 show that Jesus hates?**

The story itself is fairly straightforward, but is also so remarkable that it is well worth rehearsing. Jesus goes up to Jerusalem (v 13). He makes his way to the temple courts (v 14), but there discovers, evidently to his horror, a commercial enterprise in full swing. People are selling cattle and sheep and doves, and others exchanging money. The temple courts had become a significant place of business transaction. In response, Jesus makes "a whip out of cords" (v 15)—not a particularly dangerous or vicious kind of whip— and drives out of there these people who are making money in the temple. He even turns over their tables.

What was going on was not just that these money changers were making money out of people coming to "church." They were charging people to convert money to the temple currency in order for them to buy sacrificially pure animals for worship. The people who would have been particularly at risk from this extortionate business were those who were on the outside of the temple religion, the God-fearers who were not born as Jews, those who were not regular in the temple courts. So the point of disgust for Jesus is not money but blocking access to God.

If there is one thing that makes Jesus livid, it is fake religion that serves only the self.

• **What does Jesus passionately desire (v 17—see also Mark 11:17)?** The good of his "Father's house." The temple was where God was "at home" and could be met with, prayed to (Mark 11:17), and accessed. He passionately desires that people be enabled to meet with God.

3. **Why is the question asked by "the Jews" (that is, the leaders of the Jewish religion) a fair one (John 2:18)?**

The temple was the place of divine symbolic presence in the world. For someone to come along and clean house suggests a very high level of authority. The question they are asking Jesus is *Who on earth do you think you are?!* In a sense it's fair. What right does Jesus have to assume this kind of authority?

• **What will be the evidence that Jesus has the authority to dictate matters in the temple (v 19-21)?** Jesus, as he so often does, answers the deeper question behind the question. They ask him in effect who he thinks he is (v 18), and he replies not simply by asserting his authority but by asking in effect, *Well, what do you think the temple is?* (v 19): "Destroy this temple, and I will raise it again in three days." This temple here is not the physical temple that Jesus' critics thought he was talking about. No, the real temple is Jesus (v 21). The proof of this—and that therefore he has the authority to do what he has just done—is his death and resurrection, when the real temple will be torn down and rebuilt.

4. How can Christians today forget this and so treat other places or people as the "temple"?

You do not find access to God through a physical structure, through a temple, through a particular religious place or sanctuary. All that is needed to bring us to God is Jesus himself. The way to God is through faith in Jesus' death and resurrection.

Christian circles today are not immune from promoting the confusion that Jesus is addressing here. We tend to do it in one of three ways:

• Some make the physical church building a temple where access to God is found.

• Others make religious rituals or a certain ceremony, or a particular kind of musical atmosphere, the way to access God.

• Some make a human the point of access to God: a particularly dynamic religious leader—often a Bible teacher with remarkable gifts. It may even at times be possible to emphasize the Bible itself in such a way that understanding the Bible becomes viewed as a merely intellectual pursuit, and knowledge of it as the ultimate goal, rather than understanding it to be the word of God, given to us as the means by which we meet with God himself by his Spirit.

5. What should make you angry? Does it?

False religion that serves religious people's reputations or bank accounts or comfort, rather than seeking to bring people to Jesus to find relationship with God in him, the "temple." Often, we are too accepting of this kind of religion—or we ourselves contribute to it (see Getting Personal below this question in the study guide section).

6. Why do you think Nicodemus comes to see Jesus in the darkness of night?

He is a member of the Jewish ruling council (3:1)—and Jesus has already upset the religious hierarchy (2:18). Presumably he wants to remain hidden, not wanting to be seen, as he asks Jesus questions. Darkness and light will become subjects of his conversation with Jesus (see question 9).

7. What does Jesus want Nicodemus to understand (v 3, 5-8)?

That, respected religious teacher as he

is, he, along with everyone else, must be "born again" if he is to "see the kingdom of God" (v 3).

Jesus' teaching that a person must be "born again" or born of "water and the Spirit" (v 5) to see and enter the kingdom of God seems initially straightforward. Jesus is indicating that it is not enough for someone only to be born naturally; he or she must also be born supernaturally. But the more you think about it, the harder it is to understand exactly why these particular words, "of water and the Spirit," are chosen to make that point. The most likely interpretation, then, seems to be that Jesus is saying in John 3:5 that the Spirit must be poured out like water so that someone is born from above. In which case, both "water" and "the Spirit" refer to the supernatural work of God in causing someone who to be born again.

In verse 6, Jesus returns to the same theme, but this time he contrasts what the flesh does (clearly a reference to human natural birth this time) with what the Spirit does. In order, then, to answer Nicodemus' continued objection that to be reborn is not possible (v 7), Jesus compares rebirth to wind (v 8). This was a well-known comparison, because in Hebrew the word for "wind" and the word for "Spirit" are the same (*ruach*). Nicodemus will need the Spirit to work if he is to be born again into eternal life—but if the Spirit does work, then he can be reborn.

8. What is the way to be "born again" into "eternal life" (v 14-16)?

To see Jesus "lifted up" in his death and believe that through this he is able to give life. Jesus is teaching Nicodemus about the ultimate source of the power of the Spirit that is given to those who believe in Jesus: his cross, or in his terms here, his being "lifted up." As anyone looks at him raised up on the cross and "believes," they will "have eternal life in him" (v 15). God sent his Son to die out of his love for us, that whoever believes in him should not perish, but have eternal life. We are born again when the Spirit shows us that Jesus is God's Son and has come to rescue us.

Explore More

○ *Read Numbers 21:4-9. Why did the people face death by snake?*
They impatiently complained against God and his appointed leader, Moses, and grumbled about the rescue from Egypt which the Lord had graciously performed for them (v 4-5). By way of punishment, God sent snakes to bite them, and many died (v 6).

○ *What was the only way to escape that death?*
God told Moses to put a snake on a pole and raise it up; any of God's people who were bitten but who then looked at the snake on the pole would live.

○ *So what is Jesus saying about his death on the cross when he says in*

John 3 that he will be lifted up in the same way that the bronze snake was in the wilderness?

Like the Israelites in the wilderness, we have disobeyed God and complained against his good provision, and we deserve his just condemnation. But if we realize that we are fatally "bitten" and look with faith at the one who was lifted up and tasted death for us, then we will be healed, or saved. His death is the means of our salvation.

---

9. **How would John 3:17-21 have been both an invitation and a warning to Nicodemus, sitting in the darkness, listening to Jesus?**

- *An invitation:* Light (Jesus) has come into the world, not to condemn the world but to save it. Nicodemus has come into the darkness to see the light—Jesus' answers to him are shining light into his darkness. He is being invited to come into the light, by believing that God sent Jesus to take his punishment for him.
- *A warning:* Rejecting the one who came to save us means we still face condemnation. Verse 19 reveals the extraordinary fact that as humans we all experience a gravitational pull to the black hole of sin's "darkness." Our better instincts may long for the stars, but our evil desires, our sins, mean that we are attracted to hiding, to being in the dark, away from the light which so uncomfortably reveals our darkness to

ourselves so that what God already sees is revealed to us.

10. **Read 7:50-52 and 19:38-42. What effect does his nighttime conversation with Jesus appear to have had on this great, respected religious leader?**

- 7:50-52: The Pharisees are now set firmly against Jesus, but Nicodemus stands apart, asking them a pointed question about whether they wish to condemn a man who has not had a chance to defend himself. He is shouted down, but he is beginning to stand apart from the accepted position of the Jewish religious hierarchy.
- 19:38-42: By the time of Jesus' death, Nicodemus was clearly willing to identify, publicly, as a follower of the Lord. (There would have been no way to speak to Pilate and bury the body without it becoming known.) Wonderfully, Nicodemus appears to have been born again.

11. **If someone asked you, "What does it mean to be born again?", what would you say, from this passage?**

This is an opportunity for you to make sure that your group has a biblical grasp on the idea of being "born again." Put simply, every person who has trusted the death of Jesus to save them has been born again, since that trust is Spirit-given. Be aware of how your particular culture thinks of the idea of being "born again," and how that might differ from what Jesus says here.

12. What was Jesus' relationship with religion? How is this both liberating for us and a warning to us, in our religious lives today?

He hated a lot of religious activity! His fiercest critics (as we shall see) were religious leaders, and he was quick to tell religious teachers such as Nicodemus that they did not really understand the truth about God, and still needed to be born again.

Jesus' opposition to proud religious activity is liberating in the sense that it means that we need only know, love, and worship him. There is no religious to-do list to check off, or some standard we must reach or amount we must know. He is the "place" where we can have access to God, and his Spirit can work in anyone to bring about new birth.

Equally, insofar as it is very easy for us as Christians to elevate our traditions, our buildings, our way of doing things, etc. to the status of "religious rules," and very hard for us to ensure that we are not blocking access to God in any way, Jesus' anger in the temple is very challenging. And Nicodemus' position as a "teacher of Israel" who failed to understand the gospel message and who Jesus was should humble us, however well we know the Scriptures or whatever position we hold in our church. We always have more to learn, and we never outgrow our need of Christ's death and his Spirit's work.

3

Strange Harvest and Religious Red Tape
John 3:22 - 5:18

The Big Idea
Jesus has come to call all kinds of people—including those from "unlikely" backgrounds—to faith in him. Those most likely to reject his offer of living water are those who are more religious, not less.

Summary
This passage begins with the focus once more on John the Baptist, as he again humbly refuses to be jealous of Jesus, but instead points others to him (3:22-36).

Then the Gospel returns to Jesus and his time in Samaria, centered on his famous interaction with a woman at a well (4:4-26). Astonishingly, it is Samaria that accepts Jesus (v 39-42). The Samaritans were the despised ethnically-mixed people from the north of the country who had (the Jews felt) sold out on the true faith and interbred with non-Jewish people, such that their origin was no longer racially pure, and their religion was compromised. But they are the ones who respond positively to Jesus, while the Jewish religious leaders continue to grow in their opposition to him as he performs his second and third "signs," by healing a Roman official's son simply through the power of his word (v 43-54), and a lame man on a Sabbath (5:1-15). In the interchange regarding whether Jesus or the Pharisees are in charge of the Sabbath, Jesus raises the stakes further, claiming to be equal with God (v 17-18).

Optional Extra

Play "Two Truths and a Lie." Group members take it in turns to share three statements about themselves, one of which is a lie—the rest of the group must guess which is which. This game should reveal some surprises! Link this to the Samaritan woman in John 4; Jesus could immediately perceive her past.

Guidance for Questions

1. **When are religious rules a good thing? Are they ever a bad thing, and if so, why?**

   Allow discussion and differing views in response to this question, but take care to ensure that answers are not oversimplistic. Some Christians have a knee-jerk reaction of believing that religious rules are always bad (as though the Ten Command-ments were not God-given!); others tend to insist that we need lots of rules to protect us from the sin of the world around us. In this study, you will see that religious rules become bad when they take the place of relationship with Jesus, and/or when they prevent us from even recognizing and celebrating the way the Lord works among and beyond his people.

2. **Why do John's disciples appear to be jealous (v 22-26)?**

   They note that Jesus' disciples are baptizing more people than John, because "everyone is going to him" now that he is in the same area as John, and now that he (or rather, his disciples, 4:2) is baptizing people, just as John is. There is a strong sense of that human desire to be first and best and the center of attention—even when it comes to our ministry.

3. **How does John's response...**

   • **showcase Christian humility?**

   He quickly clarifies that his heaven-given role is not to be the Messiah, but to be "sent ahead of him" (3:27-28). He is a friend of the bridegroom, but he is not the bridegroom. This is the Christian way—to accept and celebrate any ministry that we are given to do, but never to think that we are the center of attention. A friend of the bridegroom is a privileged position but it defines us by what we are not—the bridegroom.

- **show us how we can be effective witnesses to Christ?**

Effective Christian witness begins with a negative proposition. Much of contemporary Christian witness is ineffective because it forgets this, as, essentially, we try to draw people to Jesus by drawing people to ourselves. We make ourselves attractive (or at least we hope to do so) in the vain hope that someone will come to us as we witness to Christ.

John's approach is quite different. He confesses freely that he is not the Christ. In essence, his ministry is built around a negative statement. In effect, he is saying, *Oh me? No, I'm nothing special. I don't have any particularly wonderful gifts. I'm not that important. You might not notice it, but I have my hang-ups too. I mess up. I'm not the one that is really interesting. Actually, that's someone else.* Our witness, then, is effective as we get out of the way and point to Jesus, like John (and not like his disciples in this story).

4. Where is Jesus, and who does he speak with (v 4-8)?

In (or near) a town in Samaria. While there, he speaks on his own initiative to a woman on her own at a well.

○ *OPTIONAL: It is possible that in answering question 4, your group will move on to why all this is shocking, but if not, ask: Why is this setting and this conversation surprising?*
Samaritans were the despised, ethnically-mixed people from the north of the country who had (the Jews felt) sold out on the true faith and interbred with non-Jewish people, such that their origin was no longer racially pure, and their religion was compromised. It is said that the Jews of Jesus' day would avoid travel through Samaria to escape hassle, contamination, and danger. They would take the longer route round, crossing over the Jordan and traveling through Perea. But Jesus takes the direct route.

Therefore, speaking to a Samaritan woman was not something done by Jewish males who wished to remain pure. As John notes, the woman was surprised because "Jews do not associate with Samaritans" (v 9), and especially not with Samaritan women. The point is that Jesus is in an unexpected place, having a very unexpected conversation—and all on his own initiative.

5. What does Jesus...
- **offer this woman?**

v 10, 13-14: "living water"—something spiritual of momentous importance, which leads to eternal life.

- **tell this woman?**
  - v 16-18: That he knows her situation: she is living a life of serial monogamy, one husband after another, and she is on her sixth man—this one not her husband.
  - v 21-24: There is now a new day when the gospel is going to all nations, and therefore worship does not have to take place in the

physical temple in Jerusalem. What God is looking for is true worshipers who will worship "in the Spirit and in truth." The age-old argument about which place God should be worshiped in is now irrelevant. What defines worship now is worshiping the Person the Spirit points us to, not worshiping in a particular place.

- v 26: Jesus is the Messiah, who makes things clear. He is the one through whom we can worship in the Spirit and in truth.

- **Why does she, and the townspeople, end up believing that "this man really is the Savior of the world" (v 25-26, 39-42)?**
Because he is the Messiah who "will explain everything to us" (v 25); because he knows the details of the woman's life (and yet still speaks to her and offers her new life) (v 39); because the woman tells the townspeople to come and listen to him (v 39); because of his teaching over two days, which means the townspeople believe on the basis of what they have heard from him, rather than simply on what the woman has said about him (v 40-42).

6. **What does Jesus say has been going on at this well (v 35-38)?**
A gospel harvest. In Samaria (of all places!), Jesus is accepted (unlike in his home town, v 44).

So here is the beginning of the New Testament missionary agenda and promise. The gospel is to go from Jerusalem to Judea to Samaria and to the ends of the earth (Acts 1:8). What is more, Jesus' summary of the meaning of this encounter shows us that this gospel progress is deliberately (and surprisingly) intended to be a strange harvest of great abundance. The gospel is not only for a certain racially pure group. Now it is, and must be, for all nations. Samaria needs to learn that, as does Jerusalem, and the ends of the earth.

7. **How can focusing too much on ourselves...**

- **stop us witnessing?**
If we care more for our own reputation or popularity, then we will often keep our mouths shut about Jesus for fear of rejection. It also stops us celebrating what the Lord is doing through others (as it did with John's disciples) because, deep down, we are disappointed that it wasn't us whom God used and whom others are praising.

- **cause us to witness in an ineffective way?**
You cannot point to Christ without pointing away from yourself. So witness that attempts to make us look good in some way will always fail truly to show Jesus to people. It is not effective to suggest that we are intellectually clever, or have life all sorted out, or have some amazing new explanation of the gospel. When we truly wish to become less and for Jesus to become more, then we will humbly, honestly, and boldly point to him. That is when our witness is effective.

8. Who are the people in your area who would be the strangest gospel harvest, as this much-married Samaritan woman was here? How can you initiate conversations with them, and how can you communicate the gospel to them?

We are much better at spending time with and talking to people "like us." Challenge your group to identify those whom we are tempted to avoid meeting or spending time with, and also work out what proactive gospel engagement with that group of people would look like—and ask how you will all get on with this.

9. What does this second "sign" tell us about Jesus?

Jesus' word is powerful. He does not have to be physically present to change a life utterly, simply through his word. The man's son was healed at the exact time that Jesus spoke. Jesus has total, sovereign power over sickness—and over this world.

○ *OPTIONAL: What do Jesus' words in verse 48 suggest he is hoping for?*

It seems that his words here are almost a rebuke, as well as a statement of fact—that without signs, people will not believe. In 20:30-31, John makes it clear that Jesus' signs are for the intention of giving us reason to believe. Signs have a God-given, positive purpose. However, in this instance in John 4, there appears to be a wisp of longing on Jesus' part for a world in which those signs are not necessary.

Jesus appears to wish that he would be taken and trusted on his own, without the need for the fireworks of miraculous displays of supernaturally impressive wonders. Yes, signs are given that we may believe. No, we are not to rely on the signs. We are to rely on Jesus himself. As Jesus will later say to doubting Thomas, "Blessed are those who have not seen and yet have believed" (20:29).

10. Why do Jesus' actions and words cause such trouble (v 8-10, 16-18)?

First, because he heals this paralyzed man on the Sabbath, which means both that Jesus has done "work" on the day of rest and also that he has told the ex-paralyzed man to pick up his mat, which the religious leaders count as doing "work" on the Sabbath.

Some further explanation is helpful. The Jewish leaders had learned the lesson of the Babylonian exile centuries before almost too well. Having been sent into exile for breaking the Sabbath, worshiping idols, and not following God's law, they now were determined to make sure that not the slightest infraction was committed in case it led to a fresh exile (Leviticus 26:43). They had become the Sabbath police. Rules that were intended to guard against working on a Sabbath, to proclaim the higher meaning of the Sabbath as a rest in God (itself to be fulfilled in Jesus— see Matthew 12:8), had become stringent burdens that prevented a man from being healed on a Sabbath! So they accosted the man for breaking a stipulation related to "work" on the Sabbath (Exodus 16:29), which they no doubt viewed as highly serious, and likely to provoke a repeat in Israel's history that they were determined to avoid.

Second, in answer to their accusations of working on the Sabbath, Jesus calls God his Father and points out that he works just as his Father works—i.e. that what he has done is evidence that he is equal with God. This claim to equality with God is what causes the Jewish leaders to try to kill him (John 5:18).

11. **In what sense are the Jewish leaders correct? In what way are they making a mistake?**
They are absolutely right about what Jesus is claiming—they are going to prove to be spiritually blind but they are not stupid. They fully understand that Jesus is claiming to be equal with God. The mistake is that they assume that Jesus cannot be telling the truth about himself—so, having predetermined that Jesus is not God, they oppose and plot to kill him for making that claim.

Explore More

o **What does Jesus suggest about this man's suffering and his sin in verse 14?**
His suffering and pain was somehow connected to his own sin, and Jesus now warns him to stop sinning; otherwise something worse will happen to him. (We are not told the nature of this sin, but given that the man did not bother to find out even the name of the one who had healed him (v 12-13), it may have been spiritual ingratitude).

o **What else does Jesus say about the link between suffering and sin in 9:1-3?**
Jesus says here that this man was blind not because the blind man had sinned, nor because his parents had sinned, but because the situation was part of God's design to show his glory by healing him. Physical ailments are not always the direct result of particular sins (though all suffering and pain in this world is the general result of the fallen nature of this world).

o **How should we therefore respond to suffering in our lives?**
We should ask whether the Lord may be wanting to point out a particular sin in our lives that needs dealing with. But we should not assume that there must be a link between our sin and this suffering. God may have other purposes. Certainly, given that we do not have the insight of the Lord Jesus, we are not to point to someone who is suffering and say, "You brought this on yourself."

12. **Is your church culture in any danger of elevating particular rules—perhaps made for very**

good reasons—above loving and serving Jesus?

Legalism is not, of course, to be confused with discipline. To be disciplined is like being well-trained for playing a game of tennis; to be legalistic is like creating a set of rules so that only certain very special people (a group which happens to include ourselves) can play tennis at all. Are there religious rules that we have made legalistic (not merely disciplined)? If so, the antidote, and the real point of this story, is to come to Jesus himself as fully God and find our hope, healing, and salvation in personal relationship with him, and not in any religious rules.

- **What will you do about this?**
  Be practical and specific in your answers.

4

Food That Will Not Spoil
John 5:17 - 6:71

The Big Idea

Jesus is truly God, the provider and redeemer Moses pointed to, who gives his people living bread that satisfies eternally, by giving his people himself.

Summary

The identity of Jesus—fully God and the "bread" that provides eternal and satisfying life, which cannot be found elsewhere—is again the focus in this section, which begins with a debate, moves on to the next two signs, and continues with a long discussion about what Jesus means by calling himself "the bread of life."

Jesus being God was understandably hard for the Jews to accept, for the idea of God being one was hardwired into the Jewish mindset by this time. The Babylonian exile, from which the Jewish people had only relatively recently returned, had been caused by their idolatry—their worship of other gods. They did not intend to make the same mistake again. But in 5:17-47, Jesus piles up the reasons why it is reasonable to believe that he is indeed God.

He then continues to show that he is God, through his miraculous provision of food in the wilderness—just as God gave his people manna on the way to the promised land (6:1-15)—and by walking on water and announcing himself as "I am" (v 16-21)—the name by which God had revealed himself to Moses. Here, truly, is a prophet far greater than Moses (Deuteronomy 18:15). He is himself the "true bread from heaven" (John 6:32). This is bread that does not spoil and that gives life and satisfaction forever. It is bread that is "eaten" by believing (v 27, 29), and believing is only possible if the Father enables someone to do so (v 37-40). The people are doubtful (v 41-42), confused (v 52), and finally put off (v 60, 66)—this is a teaching that is hard to understand, listen to, and accept and follow in practice. But, as Peter recognizes, these are also the words of eternal life (v 68-69)—and there is nowhere else to go to to find such "bread."

Optional Extra

"Bread-roll challenge." Take a small bread roll. The first group member tears off half of it and eats it, and passes the other half to the person on the right. That person also tears off half of the roll and eats it, and passes the remainder to the person on their right. How many people can it be passed to before the bread runs out?

Guidance for Questions

1. **What do we need in order to feel satisfied in life?**

   If your group opt for the "right Christian answer" of Jesus, then ask, "What other places do we look to day by day to feel satisfied or secure?"

2. **What does Jesus claim in 5:19-29, and how do those claims back up his argument that he is equal to God the Father?**

   To save time, you could split your group into three smaller groups, ask them each to look at three of the references below, and then have them briefly report back to the group as a whole.

- **v 19, 30**

  Jesus and the Father are inextricably intertwined in their activity. What Jesus does, the Father does, and what the Father does, he does.

- **v 20a**

  Believing that Jesus and the Father are one is possible because their unity is held together by the deepest possible commitment: love.

- **v 20b**

  The miracles Jesus has been doing prove he is equal with God the Father. The "greater works" are works compared to the signs that Jesus has completed (the third sign being the healing at the pool in verses 1-17). Jesus is essentially saying, *You ain't seen nothing yet!* There will be even greater signs to come that will show who he is.

- **v 21**

  Jesus says that the greatest power imaginable—raising the dead—is equally his as well as the Father's. Jesus will prove this later when he rises from the dead. The whole power of God is invested in Jesus thoroughly and completely—even resurrection power.

- **v 22**

  Jesus not only has the greatest

power imaginable; he also has the most fearful role imaginable too—that of judge.

- **v 23**
Jesus' equality with the Father means that the way people treat him shows how they are truly treating God the Father. If we oppose Jesus, the God we worship is not God the Father and is not the true God.

- **v 24-25**
Not only what Jesus does but what Jesus says has the power of God (as he has already proved—see 4:43-54 in the previous study).

- **v 26**
Jesus not only gives life, and not only has words of life, but he has life in his own being. He is the author of life.

- **v 27-29**
Jesus refers to himself as "the Son of Man." The "Son of Man" was a mysterious figure of divine power and authority described in Daniel in the Old Testament (see Daniel 7:13-14). Jesus uses this figure of the "Son of Man" to indicate that his essence as authority and God himself was predicted and taught in the Old Testament.

NOTE: The phrases "done what is good" and "done what is evil" (v 29) suggest to us a moralistic approach to salvation—that we are saved entirely based upon our moral actions or "good works." But Jesus has already taught in John 5:24 that salvation comes from hearing his word and believing him who sent

Jesus, and he will teach a variation of the same point in verse 40. In this context, doing what is good equals faith in Jesus. See 6:29.

3. Who are those witnesses, and how do they support him?

- **v 32-35**
John the Baptist. The meaning of verse 34 is that Jesus is not saying that John is the greatest/primary witness to the truth of his divinity (otherwise John's authority would be greater than God's). But he points his hearers to John "that you may be saved." They themselves have recognized that John is special (v 33)—they should follow his "light" (v 35) and see who Jesus is.

- **v 36**
Jesus' own miracles and signs. The signs (seven of them in John's Gospel), and ultimately his resurrection from the dead, are all designed to give them reason to believe that he is equal with God the Father (see 20:30-31).

- **v 37-40**
The Scriptures. Jesus says that the Bible—the word of the Father—speaks of him. The whole body of the Old Testament is designed to lead the one who honestly searches it and loves God to him—Jesus.

- **v 45-47**
Moses. Having mentioned the Scriptures in general, Jesus appeals to the greatest Old Testament leader of God's people, the prophet Moses.

He ends up by again challenging those who are challenging him. Moses "accuses" them before the Father (v 45). Why? Partly, because they do not keep the Law of Moses, but also in particular because Moses "wrote about me," Jesus says (v 46).

Explore More

o **Read Deuteronomy 18:15. How did Moses testify about Jesus?**

Moses promised God's people that one day, God would provide them with a "prophet like me" who they must listen to.

o **Read Exodus 3:7-10. What did God do for his people through Moses?**

God used him to rescue his people from Egypt, and then to bring that people to worship God.

o **What can we expect God to do for his people through Jesus?**

To be such a redeemer figure, gathering people to himself and bringing them into relationship with God, through his redemption on the cross.

4. **What does Jesus provide for the people, and how?**

Food that they otherwise would not have had—and notice that he provides more than enough. (There are twelve baskets left over, v 13.) And Jesus does it miraculously, using a single boy's picnic. He took the loaves from the boy, simply "gave thanks," and then the food was "distributed" to those who were seated. This is no magic trick; this is no occult power. Jesus offers a prayer of thanks, and the food is miraculously multiplied. Simple—for Jesus, that is.

5. **What is he showing about himself, do the crowd realize (v 14)?**

They realize that "surely this is the Prophet who is to come into the world." Jesus is the prophet that Moses had predicted would come, though he is far more than merely another prophet.

• **Read Exodus 16:1-16. How is Jesus re-enacting this event from Israel's time in the wilderness?**

In the wilderness, the people under Moses' leadership had no food and no way to get any—but God fed them, miraculously, with manna from heaven, promising it through Moses and instructing them on how to collect it through Moses. Here, the people around Jesus have no way to get food—but Jesus feeds them, miraculously. He provides the food they need. Notice, though, two differences: Jesus is greater than Moses because he provides the food, rather than merely passing on God's promise of that food—Jesus is acting as God, not only as God's prophet; and Jesus provides not only enough, but more than enough. There is an abundance in Jesus' provision for his people.

6. **"It is I" (John 6:20) is the Greek translation of the Hebrew "I am."**

What is Jesus claiming in verse 20?
"I AM," he says; and he was, and he is, and he is today. Yesterday, today, and forever: I AM, Yahweh, Jehovah, the Lord, Jesus. Jesus is God.

- **How does where he is standing add credibility to his claim?!**
We can imagine the scene. Calmly, without haste or worry, with commensurate ease and careful solemnity, with grace of manner and deliberate pace, the Lord's unhurrying feet walk steadily—in the midst of strong winds, miles out from the shore—on the water. A man standing on water as though it were solid ground is demonstrating that he is correct when he claims to be God.

7. **What would the crowd's two misunderstandings of the nature of Jesus' kingship—a healthcare service or an aggressive political/military leader—look like in your society or church?**
Think about ways in which it is easy to treat Jesus as someone who is simply there to fix our problems in this life; or to turn him into a political figure, with a political agenda; or to treat him as the one who will give victory after victory and cause his people never to face problems or opposition in this world. The problem with each of these is that they are never who Jesus claimed to be, or what he offered—and if we treat him in one of these ways, sooner or later he will not deliver something we think he should but

which he never promised to—and we will grow disillusioned with him.

8. **According to Jesus, what are the crowds looking for from him (v 26)? What is the problem with what they are seeking?**
They have had a good meal, and they want to keep on being fed! Their spiritual desires are really basic material desires.

But Jesus wants to redirect them away from seeking primarily for "food that spoils" (v 27). Jesus does not mean that it is wrong to earn a living—the Bible is very clear elsewhere that we must work in order to eat (2 Thessalonians 3:10, 12). Jesus does mean that they should not work merely for food; that is, they should not be fixated on material well-being.

It is necessary to take care of the body and to work for food and material survival. But this should not be the focus of our lives. Humans were made for more than the material. Jesus is calling them to a higher and more important "work." He wants them to work "for food that endures to eternal life, which the Son of Man will give you."

9. **What is true of anyone who eats the bread of life (v 35, 48-51, 53-58)?**
- v 35: They will never go hungry. Those who look for what they most need in Jesus will never find him lacking, or need to go find more elsewhere.
- v 48-51: They will never die. The

heavenly manna kept the Israelites alive, but it did not do so forever. This bread will. If someone eats of him, they will never die eternally.

- v 53-58: They will enjoy Jesus' presence with them (v 56). Again, Jesus underlines that this bread gives life that lasts forever.

- **How does a person "eat" this "bread" (v 40)?**
By looking to Jesus as God's Son and believing in him. We consume Jesus and all his benefits by placing our faith in Jesus.

- **What makes a person able to eat the "bread" (v 37, 39-40, 44, 65)?**
The Father's sovereign work, through the Spirit, of drawing/enabling people to come to Jesus in faith. Negatively put, no one can come to Jesus unless the Father makes it possible for them to do so (v 44, 65).

- **How is this humbling and reassuring?**
No Christian believes in Jesus because of their own cleverness or goodness. We are no better than anyone else, and the only reason we have come to Jesus and enjoy life from him and with him is because God made us able to. Without his work in us, we would never have placed our faith in his Son. But because it is his work and not ours, we can be confident that our salvation is secure. Jesus will lose none of those the Father has given to him (v 39).

10. How does the crowd respond?

- **v 41-42**
They "began to grumble." What offended them was that Jesus was, they thought, merely human; or rather, they knew he was human, and so they assumed that he was merely human. He was Joseph's son, they thought, and therefore Jesus could not in any sense be "from heaven."

- **v 52**
They argue about how "this man" could give them "flesh to eat." They simply do not understand what Jesus is talking about. (We may have some degree of sympathy with them!)

- **v 60**
They view Jesus' words as a "hard teaching" and wonder who could actually accept what he is saying.

- **v 66**
Many turn away from following Jesus as a result of what he has said to them.

- **Why is Jesus' teaching here so "hard," do you think?**
First, it is hard to understand. But second, it is hard to accept and follow. Perhaps they found Jesus' claims to be greater than Moses, giving them eternal bread rather than "mere" manna, too hard to accept. Maybe it was that they should not be thinking of material needs but seeking spiritual satisfaction. Maybe it was because only God could draw them into faith. Maybe it was that Jesus was claiming to be the bread of life.

11. **Why does Peter not join those who are walking away from following Jesus?**

Because he knows there is nowhere else to go—only Jesus has "the words of eternal life" because he is the only one who is "the Holy One of God." There is no other food we can find that will sustain us for eternity. Every believer has come to the point of saying, "However hard this may get, I have nowhere else to go, because only here do I find life for eternity."

12. **In what ways do we work for food that spoils? What does it look like to feed on the bread of life instead?**

Think through how our material desires or "needs" can take our attention from following Jesus, and from seeking (and finding) satisfaction in believing in Jesus and having eternal life with him. The material desires will vary from group to group and setting to setting; but there are always things that we are tempted to work for at the expense of coming to Jesus and seeking satisfaction in knowing him. Make sure your group focuses on the particular "food that spoils" they are tempted to prioritize and work for, rather than the mistakes others make.

5

Dividing Lines and Drawing in the Dust

John 7:1 - 8:30

The Big Idea

People will always be deeply divided among and within themselves about who Jesus is. But believers experience his Spirit flowing within them, and enjoy being able to be both honest about their sin and joyful about their forgiveness, extending such grace to others as they walk confidently by his light.

Summary

The Festival of Tabernacles was intended to remind Israel of God's rescue of his people from Egypt (Leviticus 23:42-43).

It is probable—and this is a key detail for understanding John 7—that there was an especial emphasis upon water. A pouring out of water was performed at the temple, and it is likely that the crowd would have recited Psalm 118, regarded as a psalm looking forward to the coming of the Messiah: "LORD, save us! LORD, grant us success! Blessed is he who comes in the name of the LORD. From the house of the LORD we bless you" (Psalm 118:25-26).

Once we grasp this basic overall context of the Festival of Tabernacles, we see why John 7:37-38 is one of the most powerful moments in the Gospel. Crowds are gathered and water is being poured out as Jesus stands up and cries, "Let anyone who is thirsty come to me and drink. Whoever believes in me, as Scripture has said, rivers of living water will flow from within them."

All the time, Jesus is dividing opinion. Even his own brothers are revealed not truly to believe in him (v 5). The crowds at the festival change their minds several times about who Jesus is most likely to be.

There follows one of the most famous parts of the Gospel, as Jesus is confronted by a woman about to be stoned to death for adultery and avoids both condemning her and condoning her sin (8:1-11). The textual location of this section here in John's Gospel has long been doubted. Suffice it to say that even if this account is not originally a part of this narrative, it certainly fits well, and seems to me to have definitely been authentic to Christ, whether or not it was originally located here or elsewhere in the Gospels. The judgment of the woman, Jesus' compassion and salvation, and the judgmental Pharisaical approach are themes that we meet elsewhere in John's Gospel, and they are masterfully interwoven here to reveal Jesus as the great hope ("the

light," 8:12) that we all need to lighten our darkness. But the darkness rejects him (v 13, 24).

Optional Extra

Hold a "balloon debate." In this activity, each group member is assigned a controversial celebrity or figure from history to represent. They are all in a hot-air balloon together, but it's sinking fast, and someone must be thrown over the side in order to lighten the load and save the rest of the people in the basket! Each member must plead their case for one minute to be allowed to remain in the balloon. At the end of the debate the group must vote on who should stay.

Guidance for Questions

1. **Who are the most divisive public figures in your culture or country? What makes them so divisive?**

   Don't let this turn into a political debate or a rant about various celebrities! Often people divide others by their actions or opinions—at other times, by their popularity or an inability to fit them into the categories each society likes to box people into. Those who don't "fit" tend to divide opinion. If your group tends to the opinion that being divisive is always negative, point out that—as you'll see in this study—Jesus was hugely divisive.

2. **Why does Jesus not want to travel around Judea (v 1)?**

   The Jewish leaders are seeking to kill him.

NOTE: This is a good point at which to underline that when John says "the Jews," he does not mean in any way to imply an anti-Semitic message. After all, he himself was a Jew, as was Jesus. John seems often to use the word "Jew" in these contexts as a kind of shorthand for "the Jewish rulers who were against Jesus."

- **What do Jesus' brothers want him to do (v 2-4)? Why (v 5)?**
  Jesus' brothers try to persuade him to go the Festival of Tabernacles. Their reason for doing so is entirely misconceived. They perceive that Jesus is a "mover and shaker." He clearly has the personality to become well-known. Does he want that or not? If he wants that, he should stop being so bashful and hiding away, and instead go up to the great festival to make a name for himself (v 3-4).

  Why are the brothers saying this? Because they "did not believe in him" (v 5). It seems they want Jesus to go public because they are not at all sure of the truth of his claims. They want him to prove it, and they doubt that he will be able to.

3. **What opinions about Jesus are on display here, and who holds each?**
- **v 12a**
  "He is a good man," say some among the crowds.

- **v 12b**
  He is a deceiver, say others among the crowd.

- **v 15**
  He causes confusion. He does not have the right kind of credentials or background to teach with such authority, say the Jewish leaders.

- **v 20**
  He is "demon-possessed" because he thinks people are out to kill him, say the crowd.

- **v 25-27**
  He could be the Messiah, since the authorities have not killed him, think the crowd. But then they conclude they must be wrong, since they know where Jesus is from, but "when the Messiah comes, no one will know where he is from."

- **v 31, 40-41**
  He is the Messiah, say some in the crowd, since the Messiah couldn't do more than Jesus has done (v 31). He does seem to be the great Prophet-King (v 40-41).

- **v 41-42**
  He cannot be the Messiah, because the Messiah must come from Bethlehem, and Jesus comes from Galilee, say others (or so they think).

- **v 46**
  Whoever he is, the power and authority of his words are unique, say the temple guards, after failing to arrest him.

Point out to your group the great amount of division between people over who Jesus is. It even seems that the same people are holding first one position, then arguing themselves out of it, and then moving back again.

NOTE: Verse 17 has puzzled some Christians. But it probably merely means that if someone really wants in practice to know whether Jesus is who he says he is (that is, it's their "will" to do "God's will"), then the evidence is sufficient to find out.

4. **How does this heighten the drama of what Jesus cries out in John 7:37-38?**

Remember all the water in the background—all the libations being poured out; and Jesus says that he is the water of life. He is the one in whom they need to believe. If they do, then springs of living water, water of life, will flow out of the heart. Amid all the disagreement about who he is, he simply says, *I am the one who can quench your thirst.*

NOTE: To which Scripture is Jesus referring? Many possibilities could be given, and it may be that Jesus is summarizing a whole thread through the Scriptures, rather than quoting a particular verse. To my mind, though, Isaiah 55:1 best sums up the spirit of what Jesus is fulfilling: "Come, all you who are thirsty, come to the waters."

• **What does he mean by this (v 39)?**
He is referring to the gift of the Holy Spirit. The Spirit, who dwells within all true Christians, connected to us inescapably by divine cords that cannot be broken, gives us a spring of living water that wells up within. This is what

happens to all who truly believe in Jesus—this life, this spiritual life, this eternal life, satisfying every desire and longing of the human heart.

5. **What do you think it means to experience the Spirit's streams of living water flowing within you?**

The important thing to bring out as you discuss this question is that the Christ-given streams of the Spirit do make a difference. Whatever it means, however it "feels," it does mean something.

• **What difference does believing in Jesus, rather than dismissing him in one way or another, make in daily life?**
When we are tired, or frustrated, or needing renewal, we will not go to other promisers of satisfaction—to entertainment or comfort of one kind or another. Instead, we will seek and find in Jesus the great soul-satisfaction that he here guarantees for those who follow him.

6. **By the end of verse 5, what two options does it seem Jesus must choose between?**

Arguing that the woman should be given mercy and not stoned or agreeing that she should be stoned to death.

• **How would either choice spring the "trap" the religious leaders have set (v 6)? What would each choice allow them to accuse Jesus of?**
With his opponents having now quoted the authority of Moses, if

Jesus does seek to rescue the woman from this judicial death sentence, he will be in trouble, as they will accuse him of ignoring the explicit demands of the law. On the other hand, if he does not—if he agrees to their accusation—much of Jesus' reputation and popularity might begin to slip away. Their quoting Scripture in defense of a deeply unpopular action lights the fuse on the bomb that must now explode in the face of Jesus—unless he can diffuse it quickly.

Explore More

○ *A good question to ask is whether the religious leaders are right: did Moses command God's people to "stone such women"?*

○ *Read Leviticus 20:10. If the religious leaders in John 8 had truly cared about Mosaic justice, who else would have been standing before Jesus?*

A man! It was indeed true that the penalty for adultery, according to the Law of Moses, was death. But again, it was for both the man and woman. This woman had been "caught in the act of adultery" (v 4), so the adulterous man must have been there when she was caught. But justice is not on the agenda of the religious leaders who have dragged this woman before Jesus.

○ *Scan-read Leviticus 1:1-9; 2 Samuel 11:1-5; Psalm 51. What did the Old Testament law provide for those who had done something*

worthy of death, such as committing adultery?

Within the context of the law as a whole, replete with sacrifices for those guilty of sin, there was remedy for sin within the mercy of God for the repentant sinner. If, according to the law, the adulterer must always have been put to death, whatever the repentant nature of their heart, then Psalm 51 would never have been written, and David (who was both an adulterer and a murderer) would never have been able to be forgiven.

7. **How do Jesus' words and actions neither condemn the woman nor condone her sin?**

Jesus says, "Let any one of you who is without sin be the first to throw a stone at her" (John 8:7). The response is that they start to drift away (v 9), as Jesus averts his gaze by continuing to write on the ground (v 8). The general point of Jesus' statement may be that no one is without sin and therefore they are unable to judge. It may be more specific—that they have been guilty of the same crime too, especially when we consider Jesus' teaching in the Sermon on the Mount, that adultery is not only physical but a matter of the eye and of the heart too (Matthew 5:27-28). Jesus (who does have the right to judge, as the sinless Son of God), will not condemn her either (John 8:11).

This has often been misunderstood to mean that Jesus does not take a stand against unrighteousness. But Jesus does not end his conversation with the woman simply by saying that he does not condemn her. He then instructs her, "Go now and leave your life of sin" (v 11). In other words, Jesus is drawing a line in the sand (is that what he was doing as he scribbled in the dirt?) and telling the woman that she is to repent and live life differently now.

8. In what sense does every human stand where that woman stood?

We are all sinners. We are all guilty of breaking God's law. Jesus is doing for this woman what he does for all repentant sinners: giving her a chance to start again, calling her to change, with no need for her to be condemned for what is condemnable, because of his death for sins on the cross.

9. What is wonderful about the image of himself that the Lord gives us in verse 12?

In a world of confusion about who Jesus is, and in which it is hard to know what it means to act wisely in difficult situations (such as 8:1-11), Jesus is the light. He shows the way. He lightens the darkness of sinners such as that woman; he shines his light to reveal the darkness of those, like the religious leaders, who use others to further their own agendas. The theological and practical meaning of this great metaphor is not spelled out in more detail, though it certainly includes purpose and eternal life within

its ramifications, the release from the darkness of sin and the promise of life forevermore with Jesus as our light. But the metaphor itself has a way of speaking about these profound matters as they reverberate within the souls of those who read about them and hear them spoken.

- **What excuse do the Pharisees come up with for rejecting his claim (v 13)?**

With barely a heartbeat allowed to pass, they come up with a caviling complaint based upon a form of religious red tape: "Here you are, appearing as your own witness; your testimony is not valid." They are presumably referring to Deuteronomy 17:6, where Moses taught that matters of truth needed to be established by two or three witnesses. But there Moses was talking about someone not being condemned to death without two or three witnesses. It is strange that they would apply this here to Jesus' claim—but they will do anything they can, and use any straw they can, to oppose the truth about Jesus.

- *OPTIONAL: Have you experienced people coming up with the most negative reaction they can think of to beautiful truths about Jesus? What does this show about sin?*

10. At what point will there be no doubt about whether Jesus is who he claims to be (v 28-29)?

"When you have lifted up the Son of

Man"—that is, when Jesus is put on his cross.

- **Read Acts 2:32-41. How do we see Jesus' words in John 7:28-29 coming true here?**

When told that they had crucified the one whose resurrection had proved that he was the Messiah and the Lord, the Jerusalem crowd found their consciences condemned them, and they were left in no doubt both about their guilt and their need for mercy. (The religious leaders, tragically, even then refused to do anything but oppose Jesus and his fledgling church.)

11. **How does Jesus guide us here to have a high view of sin, and an even higher view of grace?**

He does not condone, excuse or belittle the woman's adultery. It matters. We are not to make light of sin— neither the sin that society approves of nor the sin that those in our church struggle with (which it is far more tempting to excuse or condone).

But Jesus will not condemn a sinner if they are repentant. Our view of God's gracious forgiveness and restoration must always exceed our view of the seriousness of sin. No one is ever beyond the reach of God's grace.

- **Which do you find it harder to have a high enough view of?**

Often, it is both—we underestimate our own sin or that of our friends, and we underestimate the possibility of grace to those who are particularly "bad" sinners. Remember that there may be some in your group who, in their own lives, are all too aware of the seriousness of their sin and are unsure that grace goes further still. Do be ready to assure them of their forgiveness even as you underline the gravity of their sin.

- **How would this apply to, for example, a member of your church who has committed adultery?**

Think through how you, individually and as a church, might tend towards condoning the act, or condemning the one who had committed the action. Do remember that this scenario may be particularly personal for someone in your group, as either a perpetrator or a victim of adultery.

12. **How does identifying ourselves with the woman stop us from acting like the Pharisees? How does it cause us to love Jesus more?**

It is very hard to be judgmental and condemnatory when you have a clear view of your own sin, and a clear view of Christ's cross as being both necessary and sufficient for your forgiveness. And as we are honest about our sin and look at the sinless Savior, we grow to love him more and more (see Luke 7:36-50).

Free to See the Light
John 8:31 - 9:41

The Big Idea

Worshiping and obeying the Son of Man and his teaching is what enables us to see things as they are, and sets us free to live as we were designed to. Pride blinds people to who Jesus is and the freedom he offers.

Summary

Jesus does not just ask for commitment; he asks for full-orbed devotion, at the same time as promising those who are truly his disciples that they will "know the truth," and that "the truth will set you free" (8:32). Understanding the truth about him has a practical and personal freeing impact. We should not be those who think that "truth" is an intellectual game with no implications for real life. Quite the contrary: it is the *truth* that sets you free. Many people are bound by bonds they do not understand, and the first step to being released is for them to understand the truth of their situation and the truth of Jesus as the solution. Truth is in fact a Person, and a relationship with him is how we come to the truth. And once we trust him, then the truth sets us (at a personal level) free.

The religious Jews do not like the implication, however—namely, that they are not free (v 33). The debate finishes up centering on people's relationship to Abraham (v 37-41, 52-58). The Jews who

are rejecting Jesus are not children of Abraham, but rather, of the devil (since they are following his lies, rather than listening to truth—verses 44-45), whereas Jesus is the one toward whom Abraham pointed (v 56). Jesus' final statement is a clear claim to divinity: "Very truly I tell you ... before Abraham was born, I am!" (v 58). The resonance of the "I am" statements throughout chapters 6 – 8 now comes to a crashing conclusion. Jesus is claiming to be the "I AM," Yahweh, God, the eternal one.

There follows the next sign, the healing of the man born blind (9:1-7). But it transpires that he is not the only blind person—the religious leaders, in refusing to accept that Jesus is the one who restored his sight (v 13-19) and the implications of the sign (v 24-34), prove themselves to be truly blind. The story of the blind man being healed illustrates who "sees" that Jesus is the light (v 5) and who does not. Jesus has come that those who are blind may see (and to make clear who are truly "blind" even though they think they can see).

Optional Extra

Blindfold one member of the group. Silently choose another member of the group to come forward. The blindfolded person must try and guess who it is by placing one hand on their head. (This should be quite difficult!) Then the blindfold is removed and the mystery person's identity is revealed. When we have our eyes opened, we can, of course, immediately tell who someone is! Likewise, we must have our "spiritual" eyes opened in order to see who Jesus really is.

Guidance for Questions

1. **What does it mean to be free? Why is freedom so important to us?**

   In Western society, freedom is one of the highest goals and rights. Anything that seems to limit our freedom tends to be dismissed or resisted. At the same time, no one is completely free. (None of us are free to become an eagle!) To encourage discussion, you might like to ask your group what we seek to be free from, and free for.

2. **Look at what Jesus says about the route to real freedom (v 31-32). What is strange about it?**

   It comes through holding to his teaching. Many people are bound by bonds they do not understand, and the first step to being released is for them to understand the truth of their situation and the truth of Jesus as the solution. Such truth is not merely individualistic or self-projected—not merely my truth but the truth. Truth is in fact a Person, and a relationship with him is how we come to the truth.

   In a culture where religion is seen as constraining and rules as limiting of freedom, here is Jesus saying that the route to freedom is not to throw off the constraints of obeying him as

God but to gladly accept his rule. It is the antithesis of the world's view.

3. **What does Jesus say that all people need to be freed from, and for (v 34-36)?**
   - From sin (v 34). Addictive behaviors—the way repeated actions create channels in the architecture of our minds—are all reflective of this simple statement: that whoever sins is a slave to sin. Habits are not easily broken, and when they are sinful habits, they spiral down into slavery. We may feel we choose to sin, but in truth that sin is our master.
   - From insecurity (v 35). A slave has "no permanent place in the family." They have no certainty for the future, and cannot know they are loved or accepted. Because we are slaves to sin, we are outside the loving, secure relationship with God for which we were made.
   - For family (v 35-36). Jesus is the Son, and so if he sets us free, he brings us into the relationship that he enjoys with his Father. We are set free by Jesus to belong to God's family forever.

4. **Why does this language of slavery and freedom offend those who are listening to him (v 33)?**

   They argue that, as they are Abraham's children, they have never been the slaves of anyone—therefore they do not need to be set free.

- **How does Jesus answer their claim that they do not need to be set** free because they are not slaves, but rather, children of Abraham (v 39-47)?

Abraham's true children would do what Abraham did (v 39)—they, on the other hand, are trying to kill him. This is not what Abraham would do (v 40). Therefore, they are not really Abraham's children. Jesus does not dispute their physical heritage. He is saying that spiritually they are in slavery. In fact, they are displaying characteristics of quite a different kind of "father" than Abraham (v 41). Their father is the devil. Because they are rejecting Jesus—indeed, they are seeking to destroy him and lying about it—the only conclusion is that really they are following the instructions of the enemy of Jesus and of his Father: that is, the devil himself. They are opposed to the truth (v 45): they will not listen to Jesus. And "the reason you do not hear is that you do not belong to God" (v 47).

5. What is Jesus' relationship to Abraham?

Accepting for a moment their claim that Abraham is their father, Jesus tells them that "your father Abraham rejoiced at the thought of seeing my day; he saw it and was glad" (v 56). Jesus is greater than Abraham (v 53)—Abraham was excited at the prospect of Jesus' coming to make it true that "whoever obeys my word will never see death" (v 51). In fact, Abraham saw Jesus (see Explore More below for more on this).

• How could Abraham have seen Jesus, when Jesus is less than 50 years old (v 57)?

Jesus answers with one of the most famous utterances of his divinity: "Very truly I tell you … before Abraham was born, I am!" (v 58). Jesus is claiming to be the "I AM," Yahweh, God, the eternal one. In case any think that Jesus did not quite imply all of this, and that we might be reading too much into the text, we need only note the response of his first hearers: "They picked up stones to stone him" (v 59). They knew that Jesus was saying he was God.

Explore More

○ *Read Genesis 18:16-33; 22:1-19. When Abraham "saw the Lord" or saw "the angel of the Lord," who does he seem to have been seeing?* The answer that appears to hold most warrant is the traditional one: that Jesus is saying that these meetings were pre-incarnation encounters with him. Abraham saw more than perhaps we would have at first realized (or that he entirely realized too).

○ *Read Hebrews 11:8-19. What was Abraham gladly looking forward to?* "The city with foundations, whose architect and builder is God" (v 10). He was still looking forward to this when he died (v 13)—he welcomed the coming of the city/kingdom of God "from a distance." He did not receive all he had been promised, *but knew a day would come when he would.*

---

6. **When do you find it hardest to believe this? Why?**

All of us have places in our lives where our reasoning or feelings suggest that there is greater freedom in not holding to Jesus' teaching. It is good to identify these areas, and to think through what the "fake-freedom lie" is that we are tempted to believe. You could stop here to pray about the answers your group gives.

7. **Why is knowing "the truth [that] will set you free" good news for a relativistic society, where everyone's truth is seen as equally valid?**

Relativism leads us to be unable to say that anything is "wrong," since I am never allowed to impose my truth or moral code upon anyone else. This binds us to call evil "not evil." It is good news that as Christians we know the Person who is Truth, and who sets us free to live with confidence and clarity. And it is worth thinking with your group about how, while this is challenging and even offensive to those who have grown up being taught to be suspicious of any absolute truth claim, it is also an opportunity to show the goodness and freedom of living under Jesus' rule rather than the oppressive rule of believing truth to be fluid and individualistic.

8. **Who comes from blindness to sight, and how?**

"A man blind from birth" (v 1). Verse 5 reminds us that this is to be a physical illustration of Jesus' spiritual mission—to enable the blind to see by shining his light into their lives. The man moves from blindness to sight through the miraculous work of Jesus (v 6-7).

NOTE: Why does Jesus use mud and saliva rather than simply speaking words of healing (v 6)? This could be Jesus' way of confirming what he has already told his followers (v 2-3): namely, that this man's congenital blindness was not because he or his parents had done something morally wrong. Even though very obviously he is going to employ a supernatural solution, Jesus makes a very basic pharmaceutical paste, not because he wants the man to think that Jesus is a medical doctor (the man very clearly understands he has been miraculously healed, v 15-17), but because he wants everyone to realize that the man's blindness is not his own moral fault.

9. **What does Jesus accuse the Pharisees of (v 40-41)?**

Being the truly blind ones. If they were blind in the way this man was, then they would not be guilty of sin, as he was not (v 41, see v 2-3). But because they claim that they can see (their shocked tone at any suggestion they might be blind makes it clear they think they can see), it means that actually they are blind, and that their guilt therefore remains. They are not physically blind, but, far worse, they are spiritually blind. They cannot see who Jesus is, or why they need his miraculous work in their lives.

- **How have the Pharisees already shown the truth of Jesus' accusation (v 13-34)?**
  - v 14: The only detail they grasp onto is that the healing took place on the Sabbath—so Jesus cannot be from God, because he is a sinner (v 16), and therefore he cannot have healed this man. They refuse to see the evidence in front of their own eyes.
  - v 22: John tells us that the formerly blind man's parents' refusal to talk about Jesus was because the Pharisees had already resolved to throw out of the synagogue anyone worshiping Jesus as the Messiah.
  - v 24: They tell the formerly blind man to tell the truth, and then immediately tell him what the only acceptable truth is: "This man is a sinner."
  - v 28-29, 34: Unable to dispute the reality of the miracle or who performed it, they resort to bullying. They insult the man and rescind his synagogue membership. But the formerly blind man's answer reveals their blindness; they are deliberately blinding themselves to the reasonable implications of what has happened (v 31-33).

- OPTIONAL: *What does this episode reveal about how Jesus' followers can expect to be treated, often by the religious establishment?*
  The man who had experienced Jesus' sight-giving power was thrown out of the synagogue by the religious leaders because he told the truth about what had happened to him. In such a highly religious society, he would now be a pariah, alone and friendless. In this way, he serves as an example of what it means to follow Jesus—to experience the joy of his saving work in us, giving us spiritual sight, but equally to be insulted, mocked, and shut out by those who have no room for (and feel no need for) Jesus as the Son of God.

10. **What does spiritual sight look like (v 35-38)?**
   - Asking Jesus for truth (v 36—how different from the attitude of the Pharisees, who refuse to listen to anything Jesus says!).
   - v 38: Worshiping Jesus as the Son of Man.

11. **How do we spot if we are in danger of the spiritual pride that can blind us to truly seeing, and experiencing, God?**
   The great 18th-century American preacher Jonathan Edwards put it like this: "One under the influence of spiritual pride is more apt to instruct others than to inquire for himself, and naturally puts on the airs of a master. Whereas one that is full of pure humility, naturally has on the

air of a disciple" (*Some Thoughts on the Revival*, Vol. I, p. 402). The religious leaders here refuse to be instructed. But the most important quality of a faithful (and humble) Bible teacher, as well as student, is the willingness—in fact the desire, the longing—to learn. If we do not have that desire to learn and the willingness to let Jesus show us where we are wrong or ignorant—and if we are unable to listen well to those, like the blind man, who seem to have an understanding of Jesus that others around them do not—then we should be concerned that we have become proud.

12. **Is it possible to overvalue intellectual capacity and knowing the Bible? What might this look like in your church?**

There is a big difference between prizing knowledge of God's word in order to know God's Son better and idolizing knowledge of God's word in order to feel good and be known as wise. Ultimately, what matters is knowing Jesus: "seeing" him, even if there is much we do not know. (Notice that the formerly blind man was willing to admit that he did not know things during his conversation with the Pharisees.) We may know much, or think we do—and we may be very clever and well educated—but so were the Pharisees, and they were completely blind. Think about who is most respected in your church: is it the one who knows the most and can quote cross-references and has a degree from a top university, or is it the one who humbly loves and serves Jesus?

7

The Controversial Shepherd
John 10:1-42

The Big Idea

Jesus is the good shepherd, who alone is willing to lay down his life for his sheep, and lead his sheep into abundant, eternal life. His sheep are those who listen to his voice and follow him.

Summary

This is one of the most familiar scenes, and analogies, in the Bible: Jesus as the good shepherd. It is a beautiful picture; a shepherd looking after sheep is a romanticized scene in many cultures and societies. However, though it is indeed a beautiful scene, it is also a costly one.

In fact, that issue of cost, in particular of sacrifice, is right at the heart of what Jesus is saying. The good shepherd is one who lays down his life for the sheep (10:11, 15, 17-18). That distinctive attribute is the key to us understanding the meaning of the passage, rather than its pastoral sweetness merely resonating with us.

In the Bible before Jesus, the single most famous shepherd was King David. "Shepherd" does not merely mean a hard-working farmhand or cowboy type; it means royalty. Speaking of the shepherd, Jesus is saying that he is the King, but a sacrificial shepherd-king—the good shepherd, who lays down his life for the sheep.

In the second half of this passage, Jesus is first in Jerusalem for the Festival of Dedication (v 22-39), and then moves "across the Jordan" (v 40-42), away from the elite of the temple. Ironically, it is here—and not in the temple—where people come to believe in him (v 42). Jesus' sheep are those who listen to his voice (v 16, 27), not those we might expect or assume.

Optional Extra

To help give context to Jesus' description of himself and his sheep, show your group a video of sheep responding to their shepherd's voice. Just search for "sheep following shepherd" on YouTube, or find the video "Do sheep only obey their master's voice?" (youtu.be/e45dVgWgV64).

Guidance for Questions

1. **What makes someone a good shepherd?**
   - **How would you sum up what sheep are like, in three words?**
   Feel free to allow answers to range from serious to comic! You could return to this question after question 10, asking, "What makes Jesus a good shepherd?" and "How would you sum up yourself as one of his sheep, in three words?"

2. **What kinds of people enter sheep pens, and how do the sheep respond differently to those people (v 1-5)?**
   - v 1, 5: A thief and a robber, who "climbs in by some other way" other than the gate. The sheep will not follow a stranger's voice. In fact, they run away from them.
   - v 2-3: The shepherd of these sheep, whose voice the sheep listen to and whose lead the sheep follow.
   - v 3: The gatekeeper, who opens the gate for the shepherd.

   - **Who do you think each person represents?**
     - The thief: It is crucial to remember the context. The man born blind has just been thrown out of the synagogue (9:34). So here, Jesus is saying that actually the Pharisees are really not the rightful shepherds. They are wrongly trying to take over the sheep, and by behaving in such a way toward this ex-blind man, one of their own sheep, they

are revealing their true nature as thieves.

- The good shepherd: Jesus (see 10:14).
- The gatekeeper: It is tempting to wonder (though it certainly cannot be proved) whether the gatekeeper is actually the man born blind. He now sees Jesus for who he is, so he could be the one who watches for him, and witnesses about him (9:35-39). Or it could be John the Baptist; or the Holy Spirit, opening the door of people's hearts to the ministry of Christ; or it could be that this "gatekeeper" is merely part of the "coloring in" of the illustration that Jesus is using to make the metaphor more vivid and lifelike.

3. What does Jesus promise to sheep who enter "through me" (v 7-10)?

To enter through him—to believe in him—is the way to be saved, and to carry on in a healthy and growing relationship with God; you "go in and out" through Jesus and "find pasture." You never move beyond Jesus or grow out of Jesus, but he gets bigger and more impressive (from your perspective). As the trials you face become more challenging, so he grows by comparison, and you go in and out through him, constantly feeding on his word and growing in your faith in him.

The point is that "the thief [the religious leaders who oppose Jesus and look only for their own status and power] comes only to steal and kill

and destroy; I have come that they may have life, and have it to the full" (v 10).

Jesus' goal for his followers (those who enter through him, "the gate") is that they would have life—but not just be alive forever in some extended existence of the mediocre or moderately fulfilling. No, he has come to give us life "to the full" or "abundantly" (ESV). The word for "abundantly" has almost the sense of "excessively." The lives of Christ's sheep will not just be middling; they will be extravagantly, expensively, expansively full. Not easy—but full.

4. In what ways is Jesus a "good" shepherd (v 11-18)?

- He "lays down his life for the sheep" (v 11, 15, 17, 18). Jesus' death is "for" the sheep: that is, it is "on account of" or "in place of" or "instead of" or "as a substitute for" the sheep. But we do not need to consult our Greek lexicons to establish this meaning. The point here is that the good shepherd puts his body on the line to protect the sheep from the wolf. He is willing to risk his life, and (as John will later show us) actually sacrifice his life to save his sheep.
- He gathers his sheep. The "other sheep" from outside "this sheep pen" (v 16) are traditionally thought to mean those that would be reached through the Gentile mission, in line with Jesus' desire that all nations would become

one as part of his flock. Jesus has already set an example of this by his ministry in Samaria in John 4.

- **What characterizes Jesus' sheep (v 11-18)?**
  - They know him (v 14) in the same intimate way that the Son knows the Father (v 15).
  - They listen to his voice (v 16).

5. **What is both humbling and wonderful about being a sheep of the good shepherd? In what situations will this be particularly comforting?**
You are a sheep—a silly, aimless, directionless, wandering sheep. Even the best of us is still a mere sheep. This truth calls you to dependence on Jesus, to listening to his voice, and to following him. But such a humbling realization, which none of us in our honest moments are very far from admitting, is met with a gracious vision of Jesus as this good shepherd, who lays down his life for the sheep. We have a shepherd, and we find him faithful, true, protecting, saving, and suffering for our sake. When we do not know what decision to make, or we feel weak or under attack, or we are aware of our sin or face death or loneliness—at those moments, knowing that our shepherd laid down his life for us and he calls us on and gives us pasture is hugely comforting.

6. **How do we, as Jesus' sheep, hear his voice?**
The best possible answer is: through the voice of the Scriptures. Because

all Scripture is God-breathed (2 Timothy 3:16) and because Jesus is God, all Scripture is Jesus speaking to us. So the sheep of Jesus will be marked by a characteristic desire to read the Bible, hear the Bible taught, and understand the Bible—not because they are literary eggheads but because they want to hear the voice of the good shepherd. So creation and our conscience are ways in which we "hear" Jesus' voice (Romans 1:20; 2:15)—but supremely it is through his word to us.

The precise manner in which the Spirit communicates the voice of the shepherd to us is controversial in evangelical circles, but all acknowledge that in one way or another the Spirit empowers, convicts, convinces, softens, awakens, counsels, encourages, illumines and points to Jesus. The Spirit of Jesus speaks to us as we hear Jesus speak to us in his word.

7. **Where is Jesus now in these verses, and what is he there for (v 22-23)?**
In Jerusalem for the "Festival of Dedication." He is walking through Solomon's Colonnade, a large covered porch traditionally thought to have stood since the time of Solomon—probably because "it was winter" and this was a shelter against the wind and cold. This festival is now commonly known as Hanukkah.

8. **Why can't the religious leaders realize that Jesus is the Messiah (v 25-26)?**
Because they do not believe in him,

because they are not his sheep. So they see his works (most recently, the healing of the man born blind), but they do not understand what those tell them about who Jesus is, because they will not believe—and so they show themselves not to be his sheep.

9. **What does Jesus promise about his sheep (v 28-30)?**

"I give them eternal life, and they shall never perish; no one will snatch them out of my hand" (v 28). Eternal life is a gift. It is genuinely eternal ("they shall never perish"), and it is unchangeable ("no one will snatch them out of my hand"). Waves of relief roll over the disciples of Jesus: they are saved, and they are safe, forever. No trauma, no tragedy, no mountain, no valley can harm us. Rail and shout as the devil may, we are safe in Jesus' tender grasp. And we are safe because God has given Jesus his sheep (v 29); no one can take them away because the Father is the Father God, and he is "greater than all."

Explore More

○ *How does Jesus answer the charge (v 34-36)?*

By quoting from Psalm 82. He seems to be arguing that God says to his people's leaders, "You are 'gods,'" and so it should not be too surprising that God says of Jesus (and Jesus says of himself) that he is God. This has appeared rather cryptic to many readers, but Jesus says the "Scripture cannot be set aside"—this strange text in Psalm 82 must be true, because it is found in the Bible.

○ *Read Psalm 82. Who are the "gods" of verse 6?*

They are the rulers of Israel—in Jesus' day, the Pharisees.

○ *Why will they "fall like every other ruler" (v 2, 5)?*

Because of the way they have acted and behaved.

○ *Why should Jesus, who is claiming something even greater, be believed (John 10:37-38)?*

Because Jesus' works prove who he is, whereas the works of the Pharisees are not fitting for those who are "gods." Those spiritually privileged "gods" never did what Jesus has been doing.

10. **Where does Jesus find his sheep (v 40-42)?**

"Across the Jordan," away from the elite "gods" of the temple and the specially religious with their Hanukkah festival, and back to where John had baptized (v 40). This particular trip to the temple has come to an end. Ironically, it is here—and not in the temple at the Festival of Dedication—where people come to believe in Jesus (v 42). John the Baptist's work (v 41) had prepared the way for people to believe in Jesus. Jesus did not find anyone at the Festival of Dedication willing to dedicate themselves to him (quite the opposite)—

but away from the centers of power and the religious establishment, "many believed" in him (v 42).

11. **During which religious festival, or season of the year, do you find it easiest to forget about Jesus and fail to worship him?**

It may be that in your culture there are festivals which demand such a level of religious activity that there is little space for worship of Jesus as one of his sheep. More likely in the West, though, it will be a secular version of a religious festival with many cultural demands (often, Christmas), that becomes a season when we are less rather than more dedicated to listening to Jesus' voice.

• **What can you do to change how you walk through that time as a sheep of Jesus?**

Be specific and practical.

12. **What has particularly struck you about the nature and work of our good shepherd?**

Ask your group to write down their answers individually, before sharing them together.

8

The Resurrection and the Life

John 11:1 – 12:50

The Big Idea

Jesus is the resurrection and the life, the humble, powerful King who came to give eternal life through his own death and resurrection to those who believe him and are publicly loyal to him. Those who oppose him only serve to further his purposes.

Summary

This study takes in five events:

1. *John 11:1-45: The raising of Lazarus,* a story that enables all of us who follow Christ—mere mortals who, unless Christ first returns, will face death sooner or later—to live life now with the kind of unbridled passion for Christ that can only come about once we have settled the most significant question of our lives: what will happen to us after we die?

2. *John 11:46-57: The intensification of the plot to kill Jesus.* The most remarkable part of the discussion is when that year's

high priest, Caiaphas, prophesies that Jesus will die for the good of the whole nation. What Caiaphas means by it is judicial murder (v 53); what God means by it is substitutionary atonement.

3. *John 12:1-11: The anointing at Bethany.* The "expensive perfume" that Mary pours out without holding back shows us what worship is—it is a lavish expression of the truth that we value Jesus more than anyone or anything else.

4. *John 12:12-19: The entry into Jerusalem.* Famously, Jesus rides into Jerusalem on a donkey. John tells us that this is in fulfillment of the prophecy found in Zechariah 9:9. This symbolism would have been apparent to all who observed it; donkeys are not warhorses.

5. *John 12:20-50: The time to be glorified arrives.* Some Greeks are in town too, and they want to see Jesus. Jesus sees this as very significant: "The hour has come for the Son of Man to be glorified" (v 23). John is beginning to move in his Gospel from the "book of signs" to the "book of glory." This will mean Jesus dying, but this is the way that the Father and he will be glorified, as the Father himself makes clear. Still, though many believe, many do not—and many of those who do still have merely a belief that will not go public or risk rejection. Jesus responds to this inadequate belief by repeating who he is, and why he has come—to be the light in a dark world, saving the world before judgment comes.

Optional Extra

If you normally offer refreshments at the beginning of your study as people arrive, play a little trick... Offer group members refreshments as you normally would, but then don't make them. Wait as long as you can, until people start to notice or make comments. Discuss: How long did they wait without mentioning it? Did they feel impatient or confused? Did your actions seem out of character? Compare this to Jesus' decision to wait two days before going to Bethany in 11:1-16. The disciples were confused, and we can imagine that Mary and Martha might have been impatient—but Jesus was likewise making a point!

Guidance for Questions

1. What phrases or euphemisms does your society use for death?
Obviously these will vary. Some examples: going upstairs... passing away... moving on... shuffling off this mortal coil... joining the angels / becoming an angel.

• **Why do you think we are often so keen to avoid simply saying, "They died and were buried"?**
Death is very final. It mocks our ambitions, achievements, and accumulations, since we take none of them with us. It is notable that even people who profess to believe that there is nothing after death still prefer to use positive-sounding metaphors rather than the cold fact of "She died." God tells us that he has set eternity into all human hearts

(Ecclesiastes 3:11)—so deep down we all sense that death should not be the end, and that it is an intruder into how things should be.

2. **What is strange about Jesus' response to hearing that his friend Lazarus is gravely ill (v 5-6)?**

Having heard that Jesus loves this family (v 5), we find that instead of rushing off to be with Lazarus, Jesus stays where he is somewhat longer. In fact, he stayed where he was for two whole days (v 6). And notice how John connects the two verses— Jesus loved Lazarus and his sisters (v 5), so he stayed where he was two more days.

- **How do verses 4 and 11-15 explain his delay?**
  - v 4: There is a purpose to this sickness; even if it leads to physical death (as it will), it will not end in final death—death in its fullest biblical sense of separation from God. To put it another way, death will not be the end of this story. Jesus knows that this way, he ("God's Son") will be seen as glorious.
  - v 11-15: Lazarus has died, and Jesus will raise him again, but he uses the phrase "asleep" (v 11) as a metaphor for physical death with the hope of eternal life. But, perhaps understandably enough, the disciples misinterpret Jesus to mean that Lazarus is literally asleep (v 12). Jesus himself clarifies (v 14-15). Lazarus has died, and Jesus is glad he was not there (presumably to

heal Lazarus), so that they may believe. Something amazing is about to happen that will increase the disciples' confidence and trust in Jesus as the Son of God.

- **What are we being told about delayed answers to desperate prayers?**

Delays are because of Jesus' love. We are not to interpret the Lord's delays as lack of care, but as because of love. God's delays very rarely feel loving—we understandably enough want answers to our prayers on a human timescale, and it is hard for us to look at life from the perspective of the one for whom a day is like a thousand years, and a thousand years as a day (2 Peter 3:9). And God's does not always give us the reason for his delays, at least not in this life. But we can turn to this story, and see that Jesus' delay allowed Lazarus, and everyone there, forevermore to be 100% certain of the resurrection of the dead. Jesus' "delayed" love is a marvelous love.

3. **What is comforting for the Christian in...**

- **v 25-26?**

These are words which give Christians much courage and boldness in the face of death. Jesus is not only saying that he has power over death, though that is true. He is saying that he is the resurrection and the life. To believe in Jesus is to live, for Jesus is life. "Life" describes the fullness of life—the life for which we were made and which in Christ alone we can experience. That life begins when we become a Christian, and though we continue to live physically—a life that will end in death—our real life is now hidden with Christ in God. In that sense eternal life begins not when we die, but when we become a Christian, although it is interrupted by the painful and horrible realities of our physical death.

- **v 33-35?**

Jesus felt, and felt deeply. He knows what it means to grieve. He knows how we feel when we plumb the depths of pain and heartache. Whatever it means to be perfectly human, it does not mean an absence of feeling. So "Jesus wept" (v 35). "Jesus wept" says it all when there is nothing else you can say.

- **v 43-44?**

Jesus has the power that he claimed in verses 25-26. He can call a corpse from its tomb, and life returns to the corpse. When we face death, or a beloved Christian friend or family member faces death, we can be comforted by the fact that Jesus has not only told us that he can raise the dead, but he has shown us that he can.

4. What reactions to Jesus do we see encapsulated by the following people? What motivates each reaction?

- **Caiaphas (11:47-50)**

The Pharisees and the Council are now in a quandary. They do not know what to do (v 47-48). Their difficulty is not religious, but political. If everyone believes in Jesus, then their place at the head of the Jewish power structure—which relies on their deal with Rome—will rapidly be lost.

So that year's high priest, Caiaphas, weighs in (v 49): "You do not realize that it is better for you that one man die for the people than that the whole nation perish" (v 50). He wants Jesus to die, and his motive is the sake of the nation—by which he means at best that he is concerned about an uprising which the Romans would crush; or more likely he means that his position and that of his friends, ruling their nation under the Romans, is being threatened by Jesus. Whichever, he is convinced that judicial murder is the better option.

- ○ *OPTIONAL: **In what sense was Caiaphas saying more than he realized (v 50-52)?***

John tells us this is prophecy, describing how Jesus' death would be "for" the Jews, and also for God's children throughout the nations (v 51-52). Caiaphas is not thereby said to be holy, much less a disciple of Jesus, or even to have been aware that he was making a prophecy, much less cognizant of its full meaning. As a man or woman prophesies, they do so carried along by the Spirit of God, and their words can have fuller fulfillments than they themselves can possibly realize. What Caiaphas meant by his words was judicial murder—what God meant by them was substitutionary atonement.

- **Mary (12:1-3)**
  At this banquet celebrating Lazarus' resurrection, with Jesus as the guest of honor, Mary pours nard—drawn originally from spikenard in the foothills of the Himalayas, famed as an exquisite perfume—onto Jesus' feet. This would have released an aroma of spicy musk into the air. Mary gives the most valuable thing she has to Jesus. Her motive, implicitly, is love—the love of gratitude at what Jesus has done for her family.

  o *OPTIONAL: In what sense was Mary doing more than she realized (v 7)?*
  The point seems to be that Mary is to remember what she has just done when it comes to the day of Jesus' death and burial, to encourage her that this was all forethought and foreordained, and therefore has a purpose. It is easy for us to think of our acts of service, whether financially or personally costly or both, as amounting to little significance in the end. But here is Mary, pouring out a valuable offering to Jesus, and none of it is wasted or inconsequential.

- **Judas (v 4-6)**
  Judas complains that the perfume should have been sold and the money given to the poor (v 5). This seems, at first glance, a fairly reasonable objection, and so the author, John, immediately explains that the only reason why Judas said this was because, as the person in charge of the "money bag," he was in the habit of stealing from it for his own purposes: "he was a thief" (v 6). That was his motive for complaining.

5. What is tragic, and ironic, about the leaders' reaction to "the resurrection and the life" bringing a dead man back to life (11:53; 12:10-11)?
They plot to kill the one who can raise the dead back to life; and they then plot to kill the one who had already died and come back to life. They see resurrection, and try to kill it.

6. What would it look like for you to live as Mary did? (Be specific.)
Worship of Jesus, in daily life as well as in gathered worship, is to be unstinting and express the value that Jesus has as the one above all other values; we cannot pinch pennies when it comes to serving God.

For many of us in the West, time is the most costly item we have to offer: time spent serving Jesus, whether in children's ministries or in the world of business, whether in preaching or in evangelizing, whether as a leader of a committee or a cleaner of floors. And all of the time we pour out for Jesus as we pour it into serving him is a pleasing aroma to our Lord and Master, and matters now and forever.

- **How does John 11 motivate you to live this way?**
  Jesus is the resurrection and the life. He is the one who gives fullness of life that even death cannot end. He

loves his people, he feels with and for his people, and he raises his people. He gives us far more than we will ever give to him.

7. **What does it tell us about Jesus that he chose to enter Jerusalem on a young donkey (v 14-15—read Zechariah 9:9-10)?**

The symbolism would have been apparent to all who observed it: donkeys are not warhorses. Zechariah himself makes the metaphor explicit. The king will be "lowly and riding on a donkey … I will take away the chariots from Ephraim and the warhorses from Jerusalem, and the battle bow will be broken. He will proclaim peace to the nations. His rule will extend from sea to sea and from the River to the ends of the earth" (Zechariah 9:9-10).

This is a humble king, who has come to win victory on his people's behalf and offer peace to all who will live under his universal rule.

8. **What responses to this humble King do we see (John 12:17-22)?**

- The crowd is still high on the miraculous sign of Lazarus being raised from the dead (v 17). They are telling everyone who will listen about it. It was this "sign" that now drove their attention to Jesus (v 18).

- In another unconscious prophecy, the Pharisees shake heads at each other and commiserate with one another over the fact that their plots are coming to nothing: "Look how the whole world has gone after him!" (v 19).

- Some Greeks who are in town want to see Jesus (v 20). We know, of course, that those who truly want to "see" are given sight to understand who Jesus is (e.g. 1:38-51; 9:35-38).

9. **Read 7:30 and 8:20. What is hugely significant about 12:23?**

Previously, Jesus had not been murdered by the Jewish leaders because his time had not yet come. Now Jesus declares that the time has come. John is beginning to move from the "book of signs," revealing who Jesus is and what life from him means, to the "book of glory," where Jesus will be killed but in his death glorify himself and save his people. 12:23 is a turning point.

- **What does the arrival of Jesus' hour mean for him (v 24-33)?**

  - v 24: It will bring him to his death. Like a seed that is sown, apparently dead, and then springs up alive after having been put in the ground, so Jesus will be "sown" into the ground, and through his death and resurrection there will come much global fruit.

  - v 27-29: This will be a troubling "hour," but it is also the hour for which he became flesh. And it is the hour that will glorify the Father, as confirmed by the voice that speaks from heaven. Jesus' name is glorious from eternity, and it will be shown as such at his death and resurrection.

  - It will mean that Jesus will be able to draw people from all nations to himself to enjoy his relationship with the Father (v 31-32). "The prince of this world" (a description of the one who deserves no title, the devil) will be defeated. The cross will be Jesus' victory over the forces of darkness by drawing all people to him through the counterintuitive, sacrificial power of the cross.

Explore More

○ **How did the people who had seen "so many signs" respond (v 37)?**
They still did not believe in him.

○ **Read Isaiah 6:8-13 and 53:1-3. Why do people not believe the words of the prophets, such as Isaiah 6:8-13?**
Because of blindness and hardness. There is no fault in Jesus; there is no lack of evidence. The fault is in us, in humanity, for by nature we cannot see, and will not believe, because we are blind of eye and hard of heart.

○ **Who is responsible for the blindness?**
Both us and God. We are by nature blind to the truth; we choose to be blind to the truth; and God confirms us and hardens us in this blindness. A person's rejection leads to a further inability to be able to receive; shutting the eyes against the truth in the end so paralyzes spiritual sight that a person cannot open their eyes to that truth.

○ **What does this tell us about what humans are naturally like?**
The human heart is not naturally good or liable to believe the good; it is naturally wicked and liable to be suspicious of what is right and beautiful. On our doctrines of humanity and of sin hang so much of how we live, and how we react to others.

○ **In light of this, how would people view the Lord's servant (53:1-3)?**
They would not see him as impressive or worthy of their worship. They would see him as one without beauty or majesty or attractiveness; so he would be despised and rejected, and become a man of suffering.

○ **How have we seen this fulfilled in Jesus' ministry in the first twelve chapters of John's Gospel?**
Jesus has been questioned, doubted, accused, and plotted against. The majority of those who followed him for a while did not keep doing so (John 6:60, 66). Most of the elites have rejected him and are hoping to kill him. "He came to that which was his own [the Jews, the Old Testament people of God], but his own did not receive him" (1:11).

---

10. What does Jesus say life will be like for his followers (12:25-26)?
Jesus' life and death save us, but they are also an example for us (v 25). There is an inevitable conflict: we cannot "love our life"—that is, we cannot want what we want selfishly, for ourselves—and expect that way of life to give us true life. The human condition is such that our "selves," having been made to find life in worshipful

obedience of God, are now set on a self-absorbed trajectory. Only as we die to our selfish selves can we find life as we were meant to enjoy it, in fellowship with God. We must die to ourselves to live to Christ and to find real life in him. We are following Jesus in his pattern (v 26), and like Jesus we will rise again to new life.

- **How does this reveal the inadequate nature of the "belief" we see in verses 42-43?**
Though many believe in him (v 42), theirs is not the kind of faith that is willing to suffer. They are afraid of the Pharisees, who can throw them out of the synagogue (see 9:22, 34). They love acceptance from others more than they love the acceptance of God (12:43). In the end, we all must make the same choice: are we seeking man's glory or God's; man's definition of greatness or God's; man's praise and approval or God's; man's standard of success or God's? There may be times when a lack of opposition and a comfortable life hide the clarity and necessity of this choice; but in the end we will all have to decide who we would rather have approve of us: Jesus or other people? These believers choose to prioritize the approval of other people. Their belief is not the kind that Jesus is looking for and calling for.

11. **What does Jesus remind the people about regarding the purpose of his coming (v 44-47)?**
It is to reveal God, the one who sent him (v 44-45); to be a light, drawing

people out of the darkness of sin and into the light of salvation (v 46); and so he has come not to judge, but to save. (Though he will judge one day, 5:22, he came first to save, 12:47.)

- **But what warning does he also give (v 48)?**
The words that he speaks during his first coming will judge those who reject him on the last day, on the occasion of his second coming. How we have responded to Jesus' words will be the basis of his final judgment—and, in the context of verses 42-43, the challenge seems to be not whether we accept Jesus' teaching privately, but whether we live it publicly.

12. **How would you use the first twelve chapters of John's Gospel to explain…**
- **who Jesus is? (Think of his teaching, but also of the images he has used.)**
- **what the life he offers is like?**
- **what true, life-to-the-full-bringing belief is like?**
The purpose of this question is to enjoy together the aspects of the main themes of John 1 – 12 that have most struck, encouraged, and challenged you. Encourage your group to keep their answers to one or two sentences in answer to each part of this question—and to work on their own (or in pairs if you think it would be more fruitful) and write down their answers before they share them with the rest of the group.

Bible Study Guide to

John 13–21

by Josh Moody

Josh Moody

John 13–21

The Place of Greatest Glory

GOOD BOOK GUIDE

❤ 8-Session Bible Study

Continue in John's Gospel with this second volume by Josh Moody, exploring how God's glory was revealed in the days before and after the cross.

Each of the eight sessions has a simple, easy-to-follow structure with carefully crafted questions that help you look closely at the Bible text and apply it meaningfully to your everyday life. There is also a concise Leader's Guide at the back.

Explore the whole range of Good Book Guides

thegoodbook.com/gbgs
thegoodbook.co.uk/gbgs
thegoodbook.com.au/gbgs

GOOD BOOK GUIDE

BIBLICAL | RELEVANT | ACCESSIBLE

At The Good Book Company we are dedicated to helping Christians and local churches grow. We believe that God's growth process always starts with hearing clearly what he has said to us through his timeless and flawless word—the Bible.

Ever since we opened our doors in 1991, we have been striving to produce resources that are biblical, relevant, and accessible. By God's grace, we have grown to become an international publisher, encouraging ordinary Christians of every age and stage and every background and denomination to live for Christ day by day and equipping churches to grow in their knowledge of God, their love for one another, and the effectiveness of their outreach.

Call one of our friendly team for a discussion of your needs or visit one of our local websites for more information on the resources and services we provide.

Your friends at The Good Book Company